# SPORT AND PLACE

# SPORT
## AND
# PLACE

*A Geography of Sport
in England, Scotland and Wales*

by
JOHN BALE

C. HURST & COMPANY, LONDON

UNIVERSITY OF NEBRASKA PRESS, LINCOLN

Published in the United Kingdom by
C. Hurst & Co. (Publishers) Ltd.,
38 King Street, London WC2E 8JT,
and in the United States of America by
University of Nebraska Press,
901 North 17th Street, Lincoln, NE68588

ISBNs
*Hurst:* 0-905838-65-3
*Nebraska:* 0-8032-1180-5
Library of Congress Catalog card no. 82-05-018

*Printed in Great Britain*

For Ruth, Roderick and Anthony

# PREFACE

This book was written for all those interested, in whatever way, in competitive sport, but including serious students of sport — for example, students on Sports Studies programmes. These programmes are usually inter-disciplinary, but for too long the geographical dimension has had almost no place. I also hope that the book will be read by enthusiasts who like to argue about sport and that perhaps it will help to resolve debates in changing rooms or public bars — and stimulate further debates — on where most professional footballers come from or where most cricket clubs are found.

Sport is only a recent addition to the many subjects which have been studied geographically, and although the geography of leisure is a well-developed sub-discipline, geographers have generally fought shy of a serious examination of sport. Sport and geography share an interest in regionalisation, in environment and its influence on human behaviour, in the significance of people-place attachments and in a scientific and quantitative approach. Geography can provide new views of sport, and sport for its part can provide an arena in which geographical models and ideas may be evaluated or tested.

I attempt here to explore both these avenues.

This book is no more than an introduction, since the geography of sport has barely progressed beyond the first round, let alone reached its final stages; much more work, applying the wide range of techniques, models and approaches of the geographer, lies ahead. But I hope that it will introduce students to an approach to sport that will enable them to work on their own sports-geographies as part of projects or research.

For those of us reared on the traditional names of the British counties, names like Clwyd, Strathclyde and Avon may not immediately have familiar associations. For this reason, many readers may find it useful to have an up-to-date atlas of Britain close at hand. Most of the sports discussed are familiar to readers on both sides of the Atlantic. I have used the terms 'football' and 'soccer' synonymously, and 'athletics' to mean 'track and field', but the nomenclature of all other sports should be unambiguous.

I owe a great debt to a number of people who have helped me in the writing of this book. For reasons that may not be entirely clear to them, I want to thank John Eggleston, Alistair Campbell, Eric Konig, George Reah, Andrew Huxtable, Mike Collins and Jim Riordan for their diverse forms of encouragement. Frank Elliott and Rex Walford most generously provided me with their own unpublished data on, respectively, club and county cricket, and chapter 7 could not have been written without their help. I must also thank Brian Stokes for kindly lending me his precious *Wisdens*. My frequent visits over the last few years to the National Documentation Centre for Sport at the University of Birmingham were made most enjoyable by the help and co-operation of the library staff and by many informal conversations with John Bromhead. Finally, I must thank the many secretaries and representatives of national sports organisations who have answered my requests for data. It goes without saying that while I am indebted to all these people for help, all errors and omissions are my own.

No book can be completed without the support of the author's family. I must therefore finally thank my parents for instilling in me an interest in sport; Ruth for constant help over the years; Roderick for coming with me to football matches, and Anthony for playing while I worked.

*Keele*                                              JOHN BALE
*December 1981*

# CONTENTS

# FIGURES

150 k
0                    150 k

# MAPS OF COUNTIES AND REGIONS

## COUNTIES OF ENGLAND AND WALES

| Present counties | No. on map | Pre-1974 counties |
|---|---|---|
| Northumberland | 1 | Northumberland |
| Cumbria | 2 | Cumberland |
| Durham | 3 | Durham |
| Tyne and Wear | 4 | Westmorland |
| Cleveland | 5 | Caernarvonshire |
| North Yorkshire | 6 | Yorkshire - North Riding |
| Lancashire | 7 | Lancashire |
| West Yorkshire | 8 | Yorkshire - West Riding |
| Humberside | 9 | Yorkshire - East Riding |
| Merseyside | 10 | Denbighshire |
| Greater Manchester | 11 | Flintshire |
| South Yorkshire | 12 | Merionethshire |
| Gwynedd | 13 | Montgomeryshire |
| Clwyd | 14 | Cardiganshire |
| Cheshire | 15 | Radnorshire |
| Derbyshire | 16 | Staffordshire |
| Nottinghamshire | 17 | Cheshire |
| Lincolnshire | 18 | Staffordshire |
| Dyfed | 19 | Derbyshire |
| Powys | 20 | Nottinghamshire |
| Shropshire | 21 | Lincolnshire |
| Staffordshire | 22 | Pembrokeshire |
| Leicestershire | 23 | Carmarthenshire |
| Cambridge | 24 | Brecknockshire |
| Norfolk | 25 | Norfolk |
| Hereford-Worcester | 26 | Worcestershire |
| West Midlands | 27 | Warwickshire |
| Warwickshire | 28 | Leicestershire |
| Northampton | 29 | Rutland |
| Suffolk | 30 | Huntingdonshire |
| West Glamorgan | 31 | Cambridgeshire |
| Mid-Glamorgan | 32 | Norfolk |
| Monmouth | 33 | Suffolk |
| South Glamorgan | 34 | Northampton |
| Gloucester | 35 | Glamorganshire |
| Oxford | 36 | Monmouthshire |
| Buckingham | 37 | Gloucestershire |
| Bedford | 38 | Oxfordshire |
| Hertford | 39 | Buckinghamshire |
| Essex | 40 | Bedfordshire |
| Avon | 41 | Hertfordshire |
| Wiltshire | 42 | Essex |
| Berkshire | 43 | Berkshire |
| Greater London | 44 | Greater London |
| Cornwall | 45 | Cornwall |
| Devon | 46 | Devonshire |
| Dorset | 47 | Dorset |
| Hampshire | 48 | Hampshire |

| | | |
|---|---|---|
| Surrey | 49 | Surrey |
| Kent | 50 | Kent |
| West Sussex | 51 | West Sussex |
| East Sussex | 52 | East Sussex |
| Somerset | 53 | Somerset |
| Isle of Wight | 54 | |

Maps in this book showing distributions at the time of writing are based on the post-1974 county boundaries (i.e. those in the left-hand column above), *except* Figs. 4.14, 5.1, 5.2, and 7.4. All maps that include Scotland are based on the present regions, and these are shown in the map below.

*SCOTTISH REGIONS*

| | | | |
|---|---|---|---|
| Western Isles | 1 | Fife | 6 |
| Highland | 2 | Strathclyde | 7 |
| Grampian | 3 | Lothian | 8 |
| Tayside | 4 | Dumfries and Galloway | 9 |
| Central | 5 | Borders | 10 |

# Part I
# TOWARDS A GEOGRAPHY OF SPORT

*'There is much to be done if we are to realize the vast potential inherent in the geographic study of sport'* (Rooney, 1974; 289).

# 1
## INTRODUCTION

The geographical perspective on sport is largely concerned with who plays what where. It is true that studies have been undertaken into comparative sports systems, but these have tended to be international, rather than inter-regional;[1] the study of regional, sub-national differentiation in sport is still lacking. By using the tools of analysis and the conceptual framework of the geographer, new and hitherto unperceived insights on sports may be obtained and new patterns exhumed, which, besides being of intrinsic interest, are highly relevant to an understanding of the significance of sport in society or the degree of fairness in the geographical provision of facilities. Also, myths which identify places with sports may be objectively explored.

Many academic disciplines are now involved in contributing their own perspectives to the multi-faceted study of sport. Sociology[2] and history[3] have long been interested in the subject, and more recently students from fields such as philosophy,[4] economics,[5] politics[6] and psychology[7] have shown how their approaches can bring into sharp relief many aspects of sports hitherto only hazily perceived.

Geography is a recent addition to the subjects professing an interest in sports studies. A geographical approach recognises that just as sports evolved over time, they also diffused over *space*; just as different social groups participate in different sports, so different *places* are identified with different sports; sport creates occupations and creates movement or *spatial interaction* between places; while sport leaves its imprint on culture, it also leaves its impress on the *landscape*. These italicised words reflect some of the geographers' basic concerns. Do predominantly working-class areas in the north

1

of England identify with different sports from the southern suburbs? Are minority recreational sports limited geographically as well as numerically? How geographically equitable is the provision of facilities for different sports? Can sports provide clues which aid the identification of regional cultures or regional consciousness? These questions indicate only a few of those facing the sports geographer. The purpose of this book is to begin to answer them.

There are not many words in the English language with as many definitions as 'sport'. An *Encyclopaedia of Sport*, published at the end of the nineteenth century, included references to pig-sticking as well as to football.[8] As late as 1903, a book entitled *English Sport* contained chapters on the shooting of wild stags and lions.[9] Few people would include these activities as sport today, but the word still remains imprecise. Some observers have sought refuge in the adage that 'sport is the kind of thing written about in the sports pages,'[10] but the great majority of tennis matches, rounds of golf and Sunday morning football matches receive no mention in either local or national newspapers.

The coverage of this book is restricted to what might best be described as *institutionalised contests involving the use of vigorous physical exertion, between human beings or teams of human beings*.[11] This definition allows us to consider sport at different levels of commitment, from professional to recreational, but excludes (*a*) the so-called 'field sports'[12] in which the physical prowess is more or less restricted to the animal; (*b*) activities like bowls which is barely physical and chess which is almost wholly cerebral (despite being regarded as a sport in the Soviet Union);[13] (*c*) mountaineering which may be physical but in which the competition is rather against the environment than other human beings; and (*d*) swimming with one's family on Sunday morning or on a summer holiday, or jogging around the block, neither of which can be regarded as competition — the essence of modern mass and top-level sport.[14] This book looks instead at geographical aspects of more formal sports. It leaves aside casual, non-competitive activities, which have anyway received some attention from recreational geographers already.[15]

Observers such as Edwards[16] aver that sport has nothing in common with play, but most philosophers of sport regard each as being at opposite ends of a spectrum of related activities.[17] A useful distinction between the related concepts of play, games and sport has been made by Guttmann, who suggests that organised play may be either non-competitive or in the form of contests.[18] Such contests may in turn be intellectual (e.g. chess) or physical. Such physical contests are identified by Guttmann as sports which, in their modern form, possess such characteristics as rationalisation, bureaucratic organisation, quantification and the quest for records.[19] The presence of each of these characteristics differentiates modern sports from pseudo-sports[20] such as 'Penalty Prize' and 'Superstars'.

Physical contests or sports may themselves be sub-divided. A fundamental distinction with important geographical implications is that between commercial-comsumer and participatory-recreational sport;[21] ideal models of these two types are found in Table 1.1 and to them could be added a third type, described by Lawson and Morford as 'educational-instructional'.[22] This third model is not developed here since we are not attempting to develop a latent geography of physical-educative sport (Rooney[23] and Okrant,[24] for example, have revealed the potential of this in an American context). 'Commercial-consumer' sport is more or less what Keating meant by 'athletics', i.e. 'a competitive activity, which has for its end victory in the contest and which is characterised by a spirit of dedication, sacrifice and intensity'.[25] It is frequently professional, but this is not a pre-requisite since many *de jure* amateur sports fit easily into the commercial-consumer model. Participatory-recreational sports fit more or less into Keating's definition of 'sport', i.e. 'a kind of diversion which has for its immediate end fun, pleasure, delight', and which is mainly characterised by a 'spirit of moderation and generosity'.[26] The aim is still to win, but not at any price. Such participatory-recreational sport is strongly associated with the traditional and

Table 1.1. IDEAL TYPE MODELS FOR SPORT

| | Model I. Commercial Consumer | Model II. Participatory Recreational |
|---|---|---|
| Sponsor | Private ownership and/or government | Private or by community agencies |
| Objective | To win, to profit. to propagate national interests | To experience fun of playing and contesting |
| Intended audience | Spectators who consume the contest | Player |
| Controls or government | External: coach, management external regulatory agencies | Internal: Peer-governed |
| Financial Base | Consumer-business modes: gate receipts, tax write-off, etc. | Personal fees, and indirect community subsidization (e.g. facilities) |
| Ideological base | Meritocratic | Egalitarian |
| Mode of organization | League | Fixture List |
| Participant's primary motive | Instrumental, e.g. to make a profit, to entertain | Expressive |
| Location | Localised | Widespread |

*Source:* Lawson and Morford (1979).

literal interpretation of amateur — one who *loves* sport, i.e. for its own sake. From a geographical viewpoint it is worth noting that the distribution of commercial-consumer sport is localised while that of participatory-recreational sport is widespread.

Recreational participation can take place outside the club structure, which is characteristic of serious participation. The joining of a sports club represents a degree of commitment beyond the mere desire for recreation, and helps to differentiate sports from recreation. Indeed, serious participation in sport, irrespective of a participant's level of performance, can only be achieved by the joining of a club around which fixtures or leagues are structured. For this reason, data on clubs, teams and élite participants form the basis for a geography of sport whereas most geographies of recreation have utilised sample data on participants, irrespective of their degree of commitment.

The definition of sport has been discussed at some length in this chapter because it is important to establish that this is not a book on the geography of recreation and leisure. Its aim, rather, is to provide for a major social, cultural and political phenomenon, which has been variously termed as a 'new religion' and an 'instrument of bourgeois hegemony',[27] a geographical perspective. Modern sport in Britain is important enough to claim the interest of all academic disciplines, but hitherto the involvement of geographers has been strangely limited. Why this is so need not detain us.

Because of lack of data, certain sports have been excluded from the following study. On the other hand, the author's biases have sometimes intruded so that more space is given to other sports than might appear justified. Certain minority groups too have been denied coverage. The place of sport in the lives of black British citizens is beginning to be studied,[28] but detailed data which permit any kind of geographical analysis of ethnic minorities in sport are, simply, unavailable. The main aim is to generate interest in the phenomenon of sport by the use of a geographical approach. The author hopes that his readers will find what he found in writing this book: that, in the words of John Loy, 'studying sport is often as much fun as playing sport and on occasion just as serious'.[29].

## REFERENCES

1. Varied approaches are exemplified by Rodgers (1977) and Riordan (1978).
2. A large number of texts exist on the sociology of sport, e.g. Eitzen and Sage (1978) and Coakley (1978).
3. The work of Betts (1974) is a splendid example.
4. Two of the most readable are by Weiss (1969) and Vanderzwaag (1972).

5. From the United States see Demmert (1973) and from the United Kingdom Sloane (1980).
6. e.g. Lapchick (1975).
7. A variety of approaches is found in Goldstein (1979).
8. Peck and Alflalo (1897).
9. Watson (1903).
10. Fogelin, quoted in Harper (1974), p. 249.
11. This definition derives from those of Vanderzwaag (1972), Guttman (1978) and Coakley (1978).
12. For a geographical review of these see Coppock (1966).
13. Riordon (1978).
14. Brohm (1978).
15. For example, Patmore (1970).
16. Edwards (1973).
17. Vanderzwaag (1972).
18. Guttmann (1978).
19. Not unlike modern society at large as Brohm (1978) stresses.
20. Eitzen and Sage (1978).
21. Lawson and Morford (1979).
22. Lawson and Morford (1979); see also the dichotomy of Pearson (1979).
23. Rooney (1969, 1974 and 1980).
24. Okrant (1977).
25. Keating (1964).
26. Keating (1964).
27. Brohm (1978), p. 55.
28. Cashmore (1981).
29. Loy (1975), p. vii.

# 2

# A GEOGRAPHICAL FOCUS FOR SPORT

## The major sports

There are a number of ways of ranking British sports in order of importance. Unfortunately, most of the existing surveys of this subject apply different definitions of the term 'sport' and have usually been concerned with recreation and leisure. Nevertheless, some clear-cut patterns emerge from the available data. In terms of estimated active club membership, there is no doubt that football (soccer) is, by a long way, the main outdoor sport played in Britain, with over 40,000 clubs and over a million active participants. This is followed by cricket, after which indoor sports such as table tennis, badminton and swimming are important. A tentative ranking of British sports, based on the number of clubs and affiliated active members, is shown in Table 2.1.

Table 2.1.   MAJOR BRITISH RECREATIONAL SPORTS

| Sport | Clubs (approx.) | Serious participants (approx.) |
|---|---|---|
| Soccer | 40,000 | 1,000,000 |
| Cricket | 10,100 | 410,000 |
| Table tennis | 8,500 | 200,000 |
| Badminton | 4,750 | 115,000 |
| Tennis | 2,600 | 150,000 |
| Rugby union | 2,000 | 110,000 |
| Swimming | 1,600 | |
| Cycling | 1,600 | 7,400 |
| Squash | 1,400 | |
| Golf | 1,200 | 400,000 |

*Sources:* Various.

Soccer is also the major spectator sport, nearly one-fifth of the population of Britain having paid to watch it in 1974 (Table 2.2), compared with only just over 5 per cent for the next two principal sports, cricket and horse racing. The General Household Survey[1] added the rider that over 7 per cent of the male population had watched a soccer match, and 2.8 per cent had watched cricket, within the four weeks before the interview. Sports followed on television reveal different preferences between the sexes (Table 2.3).

The position of swimming and athletics is worth noting since, as a form of pure recreation, swimming has been practised by about half

Table 2.2.   ADULTS WHO PAID
TO WATCH VARIOUS SPORTS
1974

| | % |
|---|---|
| Soccer | 19.6 |
| Cricket | 5.4 |
| Horse racing | 5.1 |
| Speedway racing | 4.7 |
| Motor racing | 4.3 |
| Motor cycle racing | 2.8 |
| Rugby union | 2.8 |
| Show jumping | 2.8 |
| Rugby league | 2.5 |

*Source:* I.P.C., 1974.

Table 2.3.   SPORTS
FOLLOWED ON TELEVISION

| | Male % | Female % |
|---|---|---|
| Soccer | 53 | 22 |
| Athletics | 27 | 20 |
| Show jumping | 17 | 29 |
| Tennis | 16 | 23 |
| Cricket | 27 | 8 |
| Swimming | 12 | 15 |
| Horse racing | 19 | 12 |
| Motor racing | 13 | 5 |

*Source:* Figures quoted in Inglis (1978).

the nation's population and 17 per cent of males participate regularly.[2] However, most swimming cannot be regarded as sport, as defined earlier. The same could be said of cycling, much of which is uncompetitive recreation. Athletics (i.e. track and field) has apparently been practised by as many as 36 per cent of the population, although this was probably through forced participation at school or in the armed services.

Sports in which human energy is less important than that provided by a machine or an animal, or at least no more important, are exemplified by horse racing and motor sports. Horse racing is watched by about 5 per cent of the population, and both speedway and motor racing by over 4 per cent. In one respect soccer does rank second to horse racing. According to Newman, 53 per cent of the adult population participated in betting on the football pools in the late 1960s,[3] but the amount of money staked on soccer is modest compared with that staked on off-course betting on horses. The former totalled £233 million and off-course betting £1,868 million, while on-course betting amounted to £275 million.[4]

## Some problems of geographical analysis

An initial problem facing a student in any field of study is to identify a conceptual framework by which analysis may proceed — finding a skeleton on which the flesh of research may be clothed. To date the most helpful framework has been provided by Rooney, a pioneer in the geographic study of sports.[5] He argues that there is a geography of every game and a sports geography of every region;[6] in other words, sports may be studied topically or regionally, a distinction clarified in Table 2.4. This book uses the topical approach, with chapters in Parts 2 and 3 devoted to the geographies of individual sports. The topical approach recognises that sport evolved geogra-

Table 2.4.   A CONCEPTUAL FRAMEWORK FOR THE
GEOGRAPHICAL ANALYSIS OF SPORT

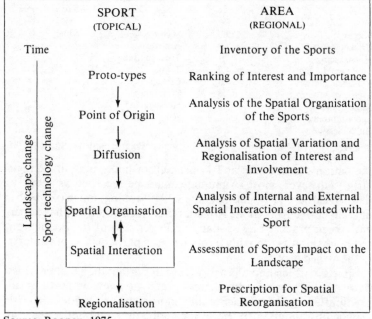

Source: Rooney, 1975.

phically as well as in time and that its present-day spatial organisation generates a vast amount of spatial interaction. In some respects this organisation and interaction is less than ideal; geographers may therefore make prescriptions for a more effective regionalisation. Attempts to produce regional geographies of sport are fraught with problems, of which the main one is the absence of comparable data for more than a small number of sports. Approaches which try to identify the sporting characteristics of particular regions suffer from several defects, each of which can be shown by British examples.

Using a small sample with rather large regional divisions, Rodgers attempted to identify the regional variations in the incidence of particular recreational sports, and to arrive at the recreational idiosyncrasies of the individual regions.[7] He found, for example, that the north was characterised by below-average participation in sports like golf and tennis and strongly below-average in cycling and athletics. The south and west, on the other hand, were above-average in athletics and 'team games'. However, by aggregating soccer, rugby and hockey into 'team games', this pioneering survey proves frustrating to the geographer interested in particular sports.

A second problem, this time concerned more with regional characteristics in terms of sports consumption, can be illustrated by market research surveys which try to ascertain the percentages of adults who pay to watch particular sports.[8] One such survey reveals that in Wales 12.9 per cent of the adult population paid to watch rugby union while only 1.9 per cent paid to watch speedway racing. By contrast, in the south-east of England respective figures of 1.8 and 6.4 per cent were recorded. At first sight these data provide some interesting information about the consumption of sport; however, no indication of frequency of attendance is given, and therefore the data need to be treated with caution. In addition, a number of *de facto* commercial-consumer sports (e.g. athletics) are excluded, and the choice of sports seems somewhat arbitrary.

A third study, using data from the General Household Survey,[9] illustrates certain methodological problems which result from the use of a small sample. The General Household Survey of 1977 asked respondents to name the sports in which they had participated in the four weeks before being interviewed, and when examined regionally it revealed, for example, that Wales contained 8 per cent of the sample respondents who played rugby but contained only 6 per cent of the population. The south-east contained 23 per cent of the sample badminton players but only 20 per cent of the population. On the other hand, Scotland contained only 4 per cent of the sample cricketers but 10 per cent of the population, while Yorkshire and Humberside had only 6 per cent of the squash players but 9 per cent of the population. These data, while suggesting certain sports preferences, again have to be treated with caution, because the total sample of rugby, badminton, cricket and squash players numbered respectively only 89, 423, 86 and 408. A shortcoming of such studies as these is that they examine sport regionally rather than sub-regionally. Differences within the north-west or the south-east, for example, are obscured by the aggregated nature of the regional boundaries. County-by-county data would overcome this problem.

If sports are studied individually (i.e. by the 'topical' approach in Table 2.4), many of the problems of interpretation described above can be overcome. Vast amounts of data on individual sports are available at county (or even city) level, which solves the problem of aggregation of data within regional boundaries; sampling problems can be answered by using a universe of data from association handbooks and the like. Varied information on individual sports is therefore ideal for a topical approach to sports geography. This is the approach adopted in this book.

However, although 'there are few activities which are as assiduously recorded and publicly recorded as sport',[10] and Guttmann

regarded precision and quantification as two of the basic characteristics of modern sport,[11] certain problems still remain, which must be
briefly noted. An initial problem arising from the plethora of data is
that different sports associations publish data pertaining to different
aspects of their activities and sometimes for different areal units.
Geographers of sport therefore need to identify which attribute of a
particular sport they are studying, and this will largely be a function
of the kinds of data available. For example, regional differences in
the provision of facilities or clubs might be identified and much work
of this type, frequently undertaken at the sub-regional level, has
already been published by the Sports Council.[12] Such approaches are
obviously vital for the equitable provision of sports facilities and
might be described as geographies of *opportunity* for participation
in sports. Alternatively, data on the number of participants or the
number of teams reflect a geography of *emphasis* on the sport in
question. Because clubs will vary in size, and because facilities will
differ in the degree to which they are used, a lack of congruence may
exist between the geography of opportunity and the geography of
emphasis for a particular sport. A third approach, particularly
applicable to commercial-consumer sports, and widely used in
Rooney's American studies, reveals geographical variations in the
number of players or athletes 'produced' by various places (i.e. born
or schooled there) — a geography of *production*. In addition,
regional differences in spectator patterns provide a geography of
sports *consumption*. Again, geographies of production and consumption may fail to correlate with each other, and with the other
sports geographies mentioned above.

There are four main sources for the data used in the present study:

1. Annual handbooks or reports of individual governing bodies
of sports associations. These frequently provide data on the number
of clubs and in some cases the number of participants, and where
addresses of clubs are provided, county-by-county tabulations and
maps can be constructed. If the data are presented by county, the
question sometimes arises whether the county boundaries used predate or post-date the local boundary reorganisation of 1974. In some
cases, therefore, the old county boundaries have had to be used. One
of the problems of using data from association handbooks is that
they fail to include clubs and members not affiliated to the governing
body. Nevertheless, it is arguable that the larger the number of *affiliated* clubs, the greater is the emphasis placed on the sport in
question at a particular place. These kinds of data form the basis of
much of the remainder of this book.

2. Handbooks containing statistical data other than that concerned with membership or club affiliations, exemplified by *Wisden*,

*Rothman's Football Yearbook* and *Boxing News Annual*. Such commercially-produced publications contain much valuable information on the location of contests and the geographical origins of élite performers. Use is made of them in chapters 4 and 7.

3. For sports in which quantifiable performances are achieved, e.g. track and field, valuable data sources are the annual ranking lists which provide information on the clubs to which ranked performers are affiliated. In the international setting, the country replaces the club as the geographical unit of affiliation. These kinds of data are particularly prolific for track and field athletics and have been used in Chapter 9.

4. Unpublished data provided by agencies such as the Sports Council and individual sports organisations and associations, following requests from the author.

5. Miscellaneous information culled from newspapers, magazines and journals.

One final problem of interpretation arising from the mapping of participants in sport needs to be briefly noted. Consider the hypothetical example of a map of participation, per head of the population, in men's hockey for the regions of England which revealed the highest *per capita* participation in the most affluent parts of the county (i.e. the south and south-east). From this we cannot infer that within southern England it is necessarily the most affluent individuals who actually play hockey, since this would involve making an inference from one level of geographical scale (the regional) to another (the individual). For this reason, the reader should not be too hasty in jumping to conclusions from the maps which follow.

This chapter has touched briefly on several problems encountered in the geographical study of sports. A conceptual framework has been identified and the wide range of data sources which are available for a geographical perspective on sports has been exemplified. It is regretted that suitable data are unavailable for an examination of each of the hundred or so sports which exist in Britain, but it is hoped that in time comprehensive data sets become available so that complete geographies of British sport — both topical and regional — can be written.

## REFERENCES

1. Veal (1979).
2. Rodgers (1966).
3. Newman (1972).
4. Central Statistical Office (1979).
5. Rooney (1974).
6. Rooney (1975).
7. Rodgers (1966).
8. I.P.C. (1975).
9. Veal (1979).
10. Ball (1975).
11. Guttmann (1978).
12. e.g. Horn (1975).

# 3
## SPORTS REGIONS

To the cursory observer the totality of sports involvement presents a confused and confusing spectacle. One way of imposing some sort of order on this confusion is to divide the area under study into 'sports regions'. Much of the second and third sections of this book adopt a particular kind of regional approach to sports — identifying areas which appear to relate strongly to particular sports. There are, for example, football regions, rugby regions and running regions. In some cases, such as rugby league, individual sports are only played in one part of the country and the sports region is obvious. In other cases, there are subtle gradations of sports involvement, and the identification of sports regions becomes more difficult.

Before moving on to a discussion of ways of identifying regions associated with individual sports, we will examine briefly the main kinds of region which can be identified in a sports context. Four kinds are introduced in this chapter: administrative regions, nodal regions, perceived regions and uniform regions.

### Administrative regions in sport

In sports as in most other things, the regions about which we can be most certain and which have the widest currency are administrative. The football supporter knows that Aberdeen will not normally play Carlisle because they belong to different administrative regions (i.e. sports leagues). Administrative regions are drawn up to solve certain problems in sport. The league system solves the problem of long-distance travel: while minor clubs play each other in local leagues, national standard clubs participate in national leagues. In table-tennis over 300 local leagues exist in England; in top-class professional football only two leagues exist in Great Britain — the English and the Scottish. As these leagues are also economic entities, they form a kind of spatial monopoly for their sport.

Most sports are organised on the basis of administrative regions. Problems of deploying coaching staff are solved if coaching regions are set up for which individual coaches are given responsibility. Central sports agencies such as the Sports Council can operate more efficiently and more equitably if they establish administrative regions, eleven of which exist in Great Britain. If an administrative region has proved too cumbersome to operate effectively, the sports administration in question may create smaller geographical units. A good example of pressure for such administrative reorganisation in British sport is provided by the proposal for regionalising the lower divisions of the English Football League. This, it is argued, would reduce the operating costs of clubs in the lower divisions, which are generally found in areas where potential income is limited. Indeed, until 1958 the lower divisions were divided into Division 3 (South) and Division 3 (North). The Chester Report on soccer advocated a return to this form of administrative regionalisation,[1] and this view continues to be recommended today.[2]

In North America a particular kind of administrative region is the sports franchise, i.e. the right to locate a sports club in a prescribed region. By administering geographical space in this way, spatial competition between clubs is avoided. As will be seen in the next chapter, this represents one of the basic geographical problems of modern British football (soccer).

## Nodal regions

We shall call a nodal region the area that surrounds a sports node (club, sports centre etc.) and which is tied to it in terms of its spatial organisation. In contrast to the administrative region, nodal regions are not immediately recognisable. However, in many ways they are more important.

Around many sports nodes are two kinds of nodal regions (or spheres of influence). One is of a positive nature and the other negative. Because all sports nodes possess positive nodal regions and only some possess the negative kind, we will place greater emphasis on the former. The most obvious positive sphere of influence is the 'fan region' or catchment area of a sports facility. Rooney noted: 'There are as many fan regions as there are teams. Some are small and embrace only a few people, while others associated with the professional teams include millions of followers.'[3] The Manchester United fan region is literally nationwide, while that for Crewe Alexandra covers only a few square kilometres. The sizes of nodal regions such as those described above are difficult to predict because they depend on a variety of factors, many unpredictable. For example, the weather can greatly influence sports attendance,[4] while in some places or at some times of the year other opportunities (sporting or non-sporting) may intervene and divert potential spectators. Fig. 3.1 adopts a systems approach to understanding the variety of factors influencing the average attendance (and hence size of nodal region) at a commercial sports event. While this was formulated initially for professional soccer, it is obviously relevant to a number of other sports.

While the quality of the service (i.e. game) being offered will obviously affect the size of the nodal region in which the club is located, the crowd is likely to come from a larger area when the home team's opposition is a good team rather than a bad one. Fig. 3.2 shows how the catchment area of Exeter City football club varied considerably in geographical extent, depending on whether it was playing a club near to the top or to the bottom of its division. However, such maps tend to ignore other factors which influence attendancees, and in defining a club's nodal regions it might be more appropriate to consider only the hard core of supporters — those, like season-ticket holders, who possess a relatively inelastic demand for the product (Fig. 3.3).

In addition to displaying nodal regions in the form of a map, representation can be made of the decline in the amount of interaction between two places as distance increases. For Figs 3.2 and 3.3, for example, we would expect more people to come to the football matches from nearer the towns than from farther away. The case of Reading Football Club is illustrated in Fig. 3.4. Graphs similar to this could be drawn for all sorts of sports facilities, ranging from the largest to the smallest. In some cases, however, particularly within a town, distance may be regarded as a passive factor in determining sports club affiliation. For the city of Bristol, for example, Campbell found that tennis was a highly distance-sensitive sport but that table-tennis was not. This probably resulted from table-tennis clubs being more central than tennis clubs, often in workplaces.[5]

Ideally, the number of users of a sports facility would decline with distance; over more than a given distance, sports consumers would no longer travel to a particular node, choosing either not to participate at all or to use an alternative facility. In an ideal world, nodal regions would not overlap, consumers making rational choices and using their nearest facility; in the real world of sports, however, this is not so and spatial competition between existing facilities or clubs is the result. Geographers may make prescriptions for an arrangement of sports nodes which is geographically more equitable. Applied to the distribution of swimming pools in Edinburgh, the NORLOC computer programme revealed that the aggregate travel to the present public swimming pools in the city was 42 per cent greater than to the optimal locations. Hodgart notes: 'In view of this it is surprising that the only pool constructed in the city since 1939, built for the Commonwealth Games in 1970, was sited in an area relatively well provided already rather than on the western side of the city where there are still no public pools. The location was probably chosen because of its short-term advantage of being near the stadium and athletes' accommodation used for the games, but it is hard to

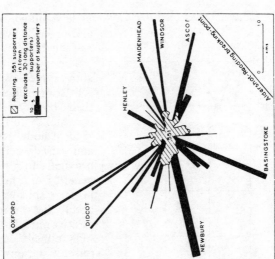

Fig. 3.1 (*left*). Some factors influencing attendances and therefore the size of nodal regions at sports events (after Rivett, 1975).

Fig. 3.2 (*left*). Two nodal regions of Exeter City F.C. The region was larger when the club played a top of division side than when it played a bottom of division side (*source*: Toyne, 1974, 20).

Fig. 3.3 (*right*). The hard core of the trade area of Reading Town F.C. (*source*: Bale and Gowing, 1976, 21).

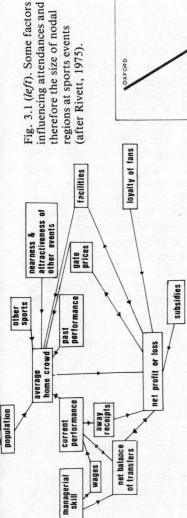

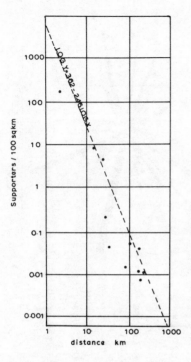

log y = 3.62 − 2.46 log x

Supporters / 100 sqkm

1000
100
10
1
0.1
0.01
0.001

1        10       100     1000
distance    km

Fig. 3.4. Distance decay function of Reading Town supporters club (*source*: see Fig. 3.3).

understand why spatial efficiency and equity were, apparently, neglected.'[6]

The nodal regions described above share the characteristic that sports consumers living within their boundaries benefit from accessibility to them. The second kind of nodal region is negative, and exists where those living in proximity to it suffer rather than benefit from their location. Such negative spheres of influence are usually less extensive than the positive ones, but they can possess well-defined 'outliers' around railway stations or bus termini. Low-order sports facilities such as village cricket greens probably do not generate any disutilities, but the impact of a professional sports club on the local environment can be serious. The greatest publicity is obtained by football hooliganism and vandalism, but traffic congestion, parking and noise should not be underrated as nuisances existing within the negative nodal regions of sports clubs.[7] For the average football club it is likely that the size of such regions is quite limited. Fig. 3.5 illustrates two such regions, as perceived by residents living adjacent to two league football grounds. This was mapped by asking respondents at each point shown on the maps to state whether the club created a 'serious nuisance', a 'nuisance' or 'no nuisance at all'. Contours were then interpolated. While limited geographically, such 'nuisance fields' ought to be totally eliminated: this could probably be achieved by surrounding sports stadia with more compatible land uses such as parking or open space so that nuisances would be confined within the internal-stadia. This might be best achieved in suburban locations, since in lower residential densities or in open space, negative spillover effects could be minimised.

Nodal regions are functionally delimited and are found around all sports nodes be they local tennis courts or major football stadia. Agencies concerned with sports need to adopt different policies

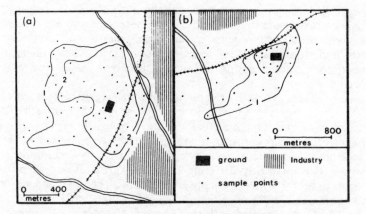

Fig. 3.5. The nuisance-fields of (*a*) Derby County and (*b*) Charlton Athletic football clubs. Nuisance contours delimit areas over which the football is perceived by local residents as (1) a nuisance and (2) a severe nuisance (*source*: Bale, 1980*a*).

towards each of the two types of region described above: the positive type should be maximised and the negative minimised or totally eliminated.

## Perceived sports regions

Just as stereotypes of sports participants differ according to the sports they play,[8] some regions are perceived as being identified with particular sports. Perceived sports regions make up the world of sport inside our heads. Each of us receives from the media various kinds of information from which we select items which form our image of particular sports. We might associate Wales with rugby union and cricket with the south-east of England: such mental maps make up part of the public's regional perception. What people *think* places are like is often more important than what they actually *are* like, since it is upon our image of places that our behaviour depends. We know little about the strengths of regional sports images, or about the degree of selectivity of media information about sport, and we know even less about what we retain and what we discard of this information. What is clear is that images, having been *communicated* by the media and *received* by the public in the form of a mental map, are often *countered* by various regions aiming to boost their image in some way. This is especially so when regions are trying to promote their image for the benefit of prospective industrialists or businessmen who might locate factories or offices there and create regional employment. Promotional literature designed to attract such entrepreneurs frequently includes references to sport: a recent advertisement designed to attract industrialists to 'expanding Northampton' included references to 'county cricket [and] racing at nearby Silverstone' among the opportunities 'you would expect and need'.[9]

It is possible to obtain a clearer idea of which regions are identified with which sports by applying to sports geography an approach first used by Green in a quite different context.[10] Mental maps of sports regions (which appear in chapters 6, 7 and 8) were constructed by presenting a sample of sixty-one Keele University undergraduate students, from widely differing home backgrounds and involvements in sports, with three maps of Britain with counties and major towns marked, and asking them to enclose with a line the area they identified or associated with three particular sports. A composite map for each sport was then constructed by placing a grid over each map and totalling the number of respondents who included each cell in the grid as part of the area they identified with the sport in question. The total scores for each cell were then converted to percentages and isopleths interpolated to produce a contour map. If such contours appear close together, there would be considerable agreement about the perceived sports region and it would possess a strong sports image; if, on the other hand, the contours were well spaced, the sport in question would have weak regional connotations.

## Identifying individual sports regions

Our fourth type of region is one described by geographers as a single-feature region, i.e. one defined on the basis of a single sport. This approach is widely used by Rooney in his seminal geography of American sports,[11] and is as near as we can come to arriving at an 'objective' regionalisation of sport to compare with the 'subjective' regions of the previous section. Depending on the nature of the data available, the present book considers regions of sports opportunity, emphasis, production or consumption (see page 10).

Following a period of geographical diffusion and the consequent adoption of the sport or sports attribute in question, a pattern of spatial distribution emerges. Certain places may be observed to have a large number of clubs or facilities for a particular sport while others have few. Some regions appear to 'produce' large numbers of élite participants in a particular sport while others produce hardly any. However, it would be misleading to designate areas of emphasis or areas of high production as 'sports regions'. This is because such absolute figures would fail to take variations in population into account. Let us consider as an example the regional differences in the provision of sports centres and sports halls. In Great Britain there are 595 such centres.[12] This represents one per 93,000 people, the national average provision. If a county had one centre per 186,000 it would have only half of the national norm. A ratio of one per 46,500, on the other hand, would represent twice the national average. Normal provision of one per 93,000 can be represented as an index value of 1.00 by using the following formula, which is widely applied below and in Rooney's American analyses:

$$\text{Index value} = \frac{\text{number of sports centres}}{\text{total population}} \div \frac{1}{93,000}$$

By using this formula we can establish an index for any county for comparison with the national norm and with other counties. The range of the indices for a given sport (or sports attribute) indicates its relative degree of concentration or emphasis within the nation. For example, a sport with a range of indices from, say, 5.00 to 0.10 would be more localised than one with a range from 1.26 to 0.87. For the sports centre example, Greater London has a large absolute number of sports centres (42 or 7.1 per cent of the total) but in relative terms has only one centre per 172,000 people — just over half the national norm. Counties with a large number of sports centres per head of the population are found in parts of Scotland, the West Midlands and Cheshire and in south-east Wales and the adjoining counties of Gloucester and Wiltshire.

If a number of high-ranking counties are contiguous, it is customary in geography to call this a single-feature region. Some arbitrary value has to be assigned, below which areas are excluded from the region, and this can create problems. Also it is possible that areas of similar *per capita* indices may not be contiguous,[13] and it can be argued that the term *areal classification* ought to be used 'to denote a subdivision established without regard to the contiguity of members of the classes while the term *region* is reserved for one which involves spatial continuity'.[14] Hence, in Fig. 3.6 two well-defined regions of above-average sports centre provision can be identified in the contiguous band of counties from Mid-Glamorgan through Gwent and Gloucester to Wiltshire, and in the group made up of Clwyd, Shropshire and Cheshire. Outliers of this region include places like Durham, West Midlands and Nottingham. This example is a geography of opportunity to participate in sports centre activities. Maps similar to Fig. 3.6 will be found in subsequent chapters.

A point of caution in interpreting the kind of map shown in Fig. 3.6 needs to be noted at this point. Where we are concerned (in

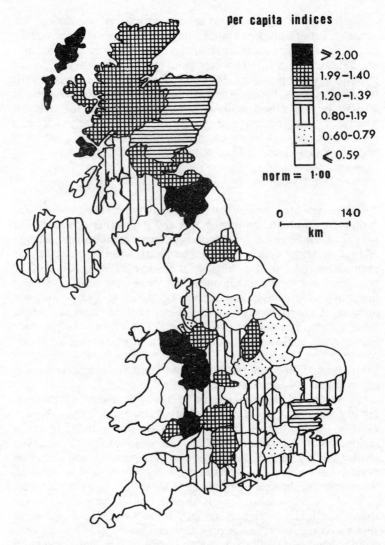

**per capita indices**

≥ 2.00
1.99–1.40
1.20–1.39
0.80–1.19
0.60–0.79
≤ 0.59

**norm = 1·00**

0 ———— 140
km

Fig. 3.6. Several regions, made up of contiguous counties with more than 1.40-times the national average number of sports centres per head of the population, can be identified in this map (*source:* Bale 1979*a*).

geographies of opportunity) with identifying areas of high and low levels of provision to participate in sport, there is the problem of treating counties (or any other areal units) as closed systems; the implication that no inter-county movement of participants takes place is clearly unreal, and the maps can only therefore be treated as a general indication of provision for anybody living at a particular place. On the other hand, it could be argued that at the *national* level, long-distance movement to sports facilities is the exception rather than the rule.

It is arguable that demographic differences between places ought to be taken into account when calculating such an index because some places contain a larger proportion of older people than others. These differences might be expected to contribute in explaining the variations in sports activity in some regions. At the county and regional level, however, extreme variations in age structure are rare and total population has been used except where stated otherwise.

A problem with the *per capita* index is that it can give a flattering impression of the significance of a sport where a very small county has only one or two clubs (teams or participants); here these small units are merged with their neighbours. Finally, in sports where the total number of clubs (or teams or participants) is small, it is best to make use of large areal units (such as Standard Regions). This has been done especially with minority sports. Rooney regards the *per capita* approach to individual sports as indicative of the emphasis placed on the sports.[15] At the same time, the *per capita* indexes, when mapped, provide a ready means of identifying areas of above- and below-average provision, participation and interest in sports. As such they may be used to compare with sports regions as perceived (page 17) and to provide information on which policies or prescriptions should be based.

## REFERENCES

1. Department of Education and Science (1966).
2. Sloane (1971).
3. Rooney (1974); see also Doyle *et al.* (1980).
4. Thornes (1977).
5. Campbell (1971).
6. Hodgart (1978).
7. Bale (1980*a*); note also Saunders (1972).
8. Young and Young (1980).
9. Advertisement in the *Sunday Times*, 14 Sept. 1980.
10. Green (1977).
11. Rooney (1969, 1974 and 1980).
12. Sports Council (1978).
13. Smith (1977).
14. Smith (1977).
15. Rooney (1974).

# Part II
# THE NATIONAL SPORTS

*'There is a sparseness, a meanness about the ground. It is like a grey snapshot from the thirties . . . the rawness of it proclaims a football town, subscribing to the male Saturday afternoon ritual which neither Women's Lib nor television sport has gnawed its way into'* (Cunningham, 1980, 15).

*'Welsh rugby is a rainy night at the end of the Llynfi Valley watching Maesteg drive forward on their table top ground . . .'* (Smith and Williams, 1980, 460).

*'We drove to Surrey and stopped at a green field, Esher Common I suppose. I saw people dressed in white and playing a peculiar game I had never seen before'* (Mikes, 1974, 47).

# 4
## FOOTBALL: PLACES, PRODUCTION AND PLAYERS

As was mentioned in chapter 2, football (soccer) is Britain's national sport inasmuch as it attracts more spectators and more participants than any other sporting activity. This chapter focuses on three aspects of football — its geographical evolution, the present-day pattern of spatial organisation of the commercial-consumer sport, and the pattern of player 'production' at the county level. Chapter 5 considers soccer as a participatory-recreational sport, drawing attention to regional differences in emphasis placed on the game and in the provision of facilities for participation.

## Origins and diffusion

The antecedents of modern football are shrouded in history and mystery. Magoun suggested that in the ninth century boys played a game that *could* have been football.[1] Until the nineteenth century, however, it was a folk-game, possessing few, if any, of the character-istics of modern sport.[2] It had no accepted rules, no bureaucracy to administer it and no records or statistics, and it was geographically unstandardised. In regionally differentiated form, however, the game was ubiquitous, being played from Scotland[3] to Cornwall.

Little spatial interaction between regions took place in pre-industrial England, and therefore local variations in style of play existed without any inter-regional competition. Good descriptions of football in its early stages have been provided by several writers, notably Dunning, Walvin, Young and Marples.[4]

Between about 1750 and 1860 a minor geographical transformation occurred in the game. In its rough form it was adopted by the private schools and universities, and because of the growing rigours of industrial and urban life, it declined in popularity as an element of working-class culture. Because the great majority of the schools and universities were located in the south of England, the game became predominantly a southern phenomenon.

A fundamental feature of the late 1850s and early '60s was the debate between those who favoured the 'carrying' game and those preferring the 'dribbling' version. The focus of the former was at Blackheath, and the dispute came to a head in 1863 when the Blackheath club withdrew from the newly-formed Football Asociation, set up to administer the sport. By and large, the soccer clubs of the 1860s were southern in orientation. Indeed, the F.A. had been formed in London, and those attending the 1863 meeting were from London and the suburbs.

The period 1860 – 80 saw the diffusion and re-adoption of the game in the north of England. Increased leisure time in the towns, associated with the arrival of the Saturday half-holiday, undoubtedly helped. A growing transport infrastructure made possible competition on a regional and national scale. The codification of rules and the formation of the Football Association in 1863 meant that a standardised game had become possible. There were active propagators of the innovation. Products of the public schools and universities 'visited or went to live in distant places and carried it with them. In this way it was transmitted from Cambridge to London, from London to the north of England, to Scotland, Ireland, Wales and then to Europe and other parts of the world.'[5] This process of diffusion seems to have been a combination of both spatial and hierarchical diffusion; in other words, football spread to neighbouring places *and*, on an international scale particularly, from economically advanced to economically advancing nations. Fig. 4.1b shows how the formation of football associations in Europe was associated with the degree of economic development; countries with a large percentage of the working population in agriculture tended to adopt football later than those where the percentage was small. Ireland was an exception, but the neighbourhood effect might account for its precocity in adopting football early in the game's international history.

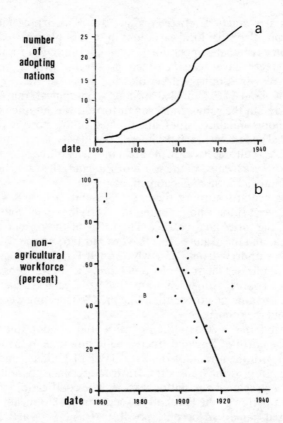

Fig. 4.1. The diffusion of soccer in Europe (*a*) *In time.* Diffusion curve for football associations in Europe. A slow rate of initial growth was followed by a speeding up in the adoption process followed finally by a slower rate as the laggard nations finally adopted the innovation. Such S-shaped curves are characteristic of the process of adoption of most sports and sports innovations. (*b*) *Between places.* Diffusion of football down the European economic hierarchy. As a rule, economically-advanced countries (e.g. B = Britain) adopted the sport before economically-advancing countries, though there were exceptions (e.g. I = Ireland) (after Bale, 1980c).

After football had become a serious competitive sport in Britain, the most successful clubs remained located in the south of the country until the early 1880s. Royal Engineers, Old Etonians and Oxford University exemplified the Football Association Cup winners in the early years of that competition — until the formation of the Football League in 1888, the only yardstick of success in the sport. After 1882, however, there was a marked northward shift in success in football at the highest level. A new breed of clubs, epitomised by Aston Villa, Blackburn Rovers and Preston North End, emerged as cup-winners and 'giant-killers'. The success of these northern and Midland clubs, located in the growing cities of the industrial heartland of England, was attributed to the fact that they had adopted an innovation in sport — professionalism. Just as football itself spread internationally in a mixed hierarchical and spatial form, so did the diffusion of innovations in the game. Fig. 4.2 shows that early professionalism was confined to the north-west and the midlands. Over time the innovation spread outwards from these areas of initial adoption, but the rate of adoption differed from region to region. For example, by 1890, professionalism was firmly entrenched in the north-east but not the south-east; the majority of midland clubs had turned professional by 1890 but in London there seemed to be a ten-year time-lag. The barrier to adoption of professionalism in the south was not geographical distance but regional peculiarities of culture and values. In the south, an amateur ethos pervaded sport. To receive payment for *playing* detracted from the gentlemanly traditions which put greater emphasis on participating than on winning. We will see in Chapter 6 how in rugby this cultural barrier was of greater significance than in soccer.

The neighbourhood diffusion described above was complemented by a form of hierarchical diffusion, though not as clearly as in the case of the international transmission of football (Fig. 4.1). While professionalism in football can in no way be described as 'trickling down' the urban hierarchy, inasmuch as large cities adopted it first, Fig. 4.3(b) does suggest that town size may have been of some significance in the decision to adopt it — and, usually soon afterwards, limited liability. The average size of town adopting professionalism in football declined after 1885, and in some regions, such as the south-west of England and South Wales, a neat form of hierarchical diffusion was clearly present, as shown in Fig 4.3(b). By the start of the twentieth century, football at the highest level had become a business, and success was measured in the accounts as well as on the field of play. At the same time the sport was contributing to, and benefiting from, a sense of 'local belonging'. 'Regular matches, local newspaper coverage, conversations with people who do watch, all these help to buttress notions of being from Bolton or Blackburn, Bury or Sheffield, Nottingham or Derby.'[6]

It was in the northern counties that several innovations in soccer were first adopted. Specialist sports papers such as the *Athletic News* enjoyed a widespread distribution, especially in the Midlands and north. By the 1890s few towns of any size in England were without their 'football special', published for Saturday evening reading; the

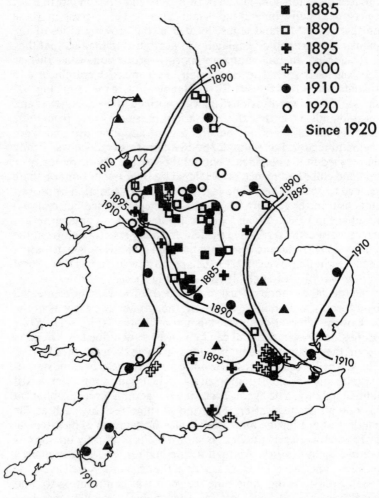

Fig. 4.2. The geographical diffusion of professionalism in soccer in England and Wales. The initial adoption of professionalism was at Darwen in Lancashire. More distant places took over twenty years to adopt the innovation. In the south of England this resistance was largely the result of cultural factors (*source*: Bale, 1978*b*).

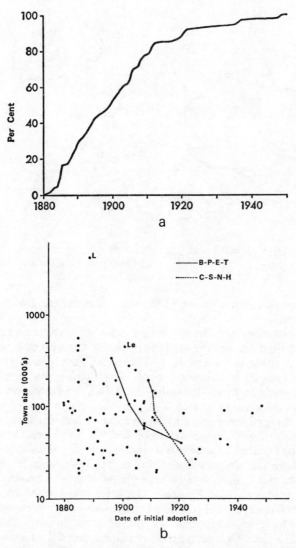

Fig. 4.3. The diffusion of professionalism in soccer (*a*) *In time*. The adoption curve for professionalism in soccer in England and Wales. (*b*) *Between places*. Scatter diagram showing the relationship between town size and initial adoption of professionalism. Town populations have been taken for those nearest the year of initial adoption. L = London; Le = Leeds; B-P-E-T = Bristol-Plymouth-Exeter-Torquay; C-S-N-H = Cardiff-Swansea-Newport-Hereford (*source*: Bale 1978*b*).

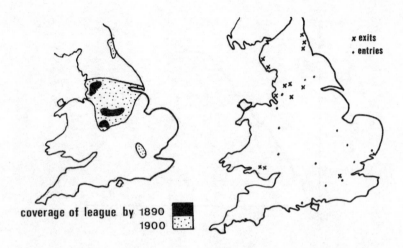

coverage of league by 1890
                        1900

Fig. 4.4. Early location of the
Football League.

.Fig. 4.5. Locational changes in the
composition of the Football League
since 1920.

first towns to adopt it (in the 1880s) were Birmingham, Bolton and
Blackburn.[7]

Perhaps a more significant northern innovation was the league: it
was recognised before the end of the 1880s that fixtures could best be
organised within this framework. The twelve founder-clubs of the
Football League, like the early professional clubs, were found in
the north-west and the Midlands (Fig. 4.4). Like professionalism,
leagues were looked upon with disdain by the amateurs of the south:
they encouraged a strongly competitive spirit which detracted from
the pleasure of sport-for-sport's-sake. By 1900, therefore, the members of the Football League had scarcely spread beyond a triangular
belt between the Mersey and the Humber; in 1898, when it totalled
thirty-two clubs, only two (Woolwich Arsenal and Luton) were
located in the south of England. The great majority of southern
clubs at this time played in the Southern League but it was recognised
that a better brand of football was played in the northern-oriented
Football League. Gradually, southern clubs joined the League. By
1910 the forty clubs in the League were in two divisions, and six
London clubs were members. Within a few years the Football
League had assumed, more or less, its present composition.

It is true that some clubs that were early League members are no
longer so. Some towns, like Gainsborough, Darwen and Lough-
borough, may have been too small to support a League team for any

length of time. In other areas there seems to have been a link between economic decline and the loss of League status. Every year, the last four of the ninety-two League clubs have to seek re-election to the League. At the same time a number of non-League clubs seek election, often using consultants to prepare and promote their cases. The clubs which have entered the League, particularly since about 1920, have tended to be in areas of relative prosperity (i.e. the south-east of England or East Anglia) or have simply replaced those in the northern areas which have left the league.

Figs. 4.2 and 4.4 show how two innovations in football (professionalism and the league) are both essentially northern phenomena in origin. A second spatial tradition in British football is its localism — to support football was to become involved in a pattern of local loyalties;[8] 'working class people could be helped to feel that they belonged to a *community* by the activities of the *local* football team and their *attachment* to that team.[9] The terraced stadium was set among the terraced houses, and 'football generated a sense of local belonging.[10]

## Recent geographical changes

In recent years several significant locational changes have been occurring in football at the highest level. It can be argued that over a period of time economic changes produce spatial adjustments in economic activities. In a sense professional football is an economic activity,[11] and changing location patterns within the game can be related to a number of economic and social trends. Each of these, and their locational implications, can be examined in turn.

1. Economic decline of the national periphery and economic growth of the south-east have, since about 1920, been reflected in the changing geographical composition of the Football League (see Fig. 4.5). Just as, in places like the South Wales coalfield and parts of Lancashire and the north-east, the corner shop and cinema have closed down, so have the local football teams failed to remain viable as members of the Football League. Of the clubs which have left the League since 1920, only one (Thames F.C.) lies outside what is known today as a government 'Development Area'. A substantial number of the newcomers to the League, on the other hand, have been in areas of more recent economic growth.

2. The growing motorway network and a more mobile population have meant that spectators can be more discriminating in the games they watch and that the old local allegiances have begun to die. Clubs in large cities have benefited from this greater mobility, but their growing dominance of the Football League has been aided by the

abolition in 1960 of the maximum wage for professional footballers. Places with large population potential have been able to generate the most income and hence buy the best players in an unending upward spiral. As Douglas put it, 'the rich clubs get richer and the small clubs stay small, or get smaller. These are the harsh facts of football life.[12] So in the 1960s three out of eighteen clubs in the north-west had a 52 per cent share of the total revenue for League matches in the region. In the East and West Ridings of Yorkshire, three out of twelve clubs earned 62 per cent of regional gross receipts, while in the north two out of seven clubs got 72 per cent.[13] Rivett revealed that whereas in 1951 about two-fifths of the total number of supporters attending matches in Lancashire watched Liverpool, Everton and the two Manchester clubs, by 1971 the proportion had risen to two-thirds.[14] Likewise, the share of the Football League receipts going to the fifteen wealthiest clubs increased from 34 per cent in 1950 to 45 per cent in 1964.[15] Wiseman sees the football industry going the same way as the cinema — fewer local outlets being able to survive and the top end of the hierarchy becoming increasingly dominant.[16] Sloane sums up the situation: 'There is evidence that a substitution effect has taken place. The growth of car ownership has meant a growing number of spectators are not tied to their local club but are prepared to travel 20 miles or so to see a First Division match in preference to a local Fourth Division encounter.'[17]

3. Very few Football League clubs operate at a profit. They tend to survive by non-footballing activities and bank loans secured on

Fig. 4.6. New entries to the Football League might more logically relocate in New Towns than remain in areas already well provided for (*source: The Guardian*, 22 December, 1976).

what are usually valuable inner urban locations. Until the mid-1950s the typical League club's income from League matches could cover the wage and salary bill of the entire club. Now it fails to cover half since expenses and travel have rocketed,[18] and in recent years several clubs have come perilously close to bankruptcy. Certain geographical trends might be expected to arise from this situation: for example, clubs might seek to relocate in more profitable areas — in towns, like the new city of Milton Keynes, which do not possess a League club but would like to do so (Fig. 4.6). Some clubs have considered doing this — Charlton have thought of relocating at Redditch in the Midlands[19] and Newport County have considered Cwmbran as a new home. However, the British football industry, unlike professional sport in North America,[20] is characterised by locational inertia. What movement has taken place among English clubs has been at the intra-urban scale, the longest move being that of Arsenal from Woolwich to Islington in 1913. However, for League clubs which have relocated within cities the average date of their last move was as early as 1907. Nevertheless, it is possible that suburbanisation of football will happen, just as it is happening in other economic activities. Figs. 4.7 and 4.8 contrast the cramped, uncomfortable site of Stoke City F.C. with that of a proposed suburban location for Leicester City. Such changes, which have proceeded with speed in the United States, would have a profound effect on the character of English football. Moving soccer to the suburbs would create a more middle-class ambience for the sport; part, perhaps, of its embourgeoisement to which sociologists and historians have referred.[21]

Another locational tendency which might be expected is that where there are two clubs in the same town they would share one ground, and thus save costs. This is a common practice on the continent of Europe, and some British clubs are known to be in favour of ground sharing. On rational economic grounds the two clubs in each of the three cities of Bristol, Nottingham and Manchester appear likely candidates, although in early 1981 it was envisaged that the south London clubs of Wimbledon and Crystal Palace would begin ground sharing at the latter's Selhurst Park following the takeover of Crystal Palace by a Wimbledon consortium.

The tendencies described above exemplify the breakdown of two of the geographical characteristics of professional football in Britain. Its 'northernness' is being eroded by the introduction to the League of clubs in newer, growth-oriented regions in the south-east; and its 'localness' has been reduced by the emergence of a more mobile and discriminating spectator. Yet in many respects football remains associated with the north. We shall explore the extent to which such associations are based upon fact.

## Part of northern culture?

A report on the football industry published shortly after the Second World War noted that 'in the north of England . . . the sound of a referee's whistle down a pit shaft will bring up a complete football team.'[22] As we have just seen, there are good historical reasons why the game should be associated with the area north of the River Trent. Although this emphasis is weakening, the composition of the Football League is such that regions in the south still possess fewer clubs per head of the population than those in the north and Midlands. Fig. 4.9 (*over*) shows the regional differences in the *per capita* provision of League clubs. Numerically, each of the ninety-two clubs of the Football League represents 534,000 people in England and Wales. So we shall take this, the national norm, as a *per capita* index of 1.00. However, the north-west and Yorkshire-Humberside both possess indices of 1.31. The East Midlands has an index of 1.28 and the West Midlands 1.14. Somewhat surprisingly, East Anglia has an index of 1.17, an above-average level of provision resulting from the relatively recent additions to the League, such as Cambridge and Peterborough. The northern planning region, as officially designated, possesses clubs at about the national average level. On the face of it, the below-average regions of the south-west (0.87), Wales (0.77) and the south-east (0.73) are those where new entries to the League ought to be located if a more equitable geography of League football is to be established. However, this overlooks the fact that the proportion of the total population which attends matches varies greatly from place to place, so that to predict the optimal locations for new league entries is hazardous. It has been noted, for example, that while 19.6 per cent of the adult population watched soccer in 1974, the respective figure for the north-west was 22.6 per cent, for the North 20 per cent, and for the West and East Midlands 21.3 per cent. Likewise, the proportion of total expenditure on entertainment devoted to soccer generally declines as one goes from north to south. Rivett has suggested that if the sole criterion were to maximise crowds at home matches, the best locations would be Crawley, Sussex, and somewhere near Dover.[23] At a sub-regional scale it could be argued that some nodal regions possess too many League clubs for their size: one of the clearest examples is the Chester region which has two League clubs (Chester and Wrexham) within 10 miles of each other in a relatively thinly populated area.

A second way of confirming the northern traditions of professional football is to look at the geography of production of professional players registered with the ninety-two clubs of the Football League. Using a sample of over 2,000 League footballers whose

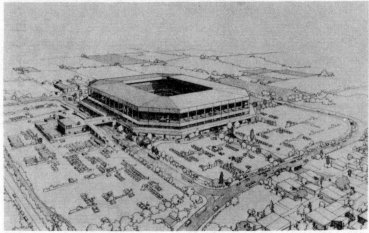

Fig. 4.7 (*above*). Stoke City F.C. in its urban setting (photo by Eileen Beard).
Fig. 4.8 (*below*). Proposed new suburban town centre integrated into a new soccer stadium. This proposed development at Beaumont Leys, Leicester, was withdrawn in 1977 but nevertheless indicates the sign of things to come.

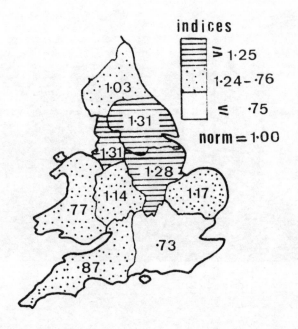

Fig. 4.9. *Per capita* provision of League football clubs,
1981.

birthplaces are recorded in *Rothman's Football Yearbook*,[24] absolute and *per capita* production figures for the counties of Britain
could be calculated. The figures described below almost certainly
under-estimate the Scottish production of élite footballers, since
those who play for Scottish clubs (several of which are comparable in
standard with English clubs) are not included.

In absolute terms six counties produce above 100 professional
players, these being the main population foci of Greater London
(276), Greater Manchester (152), Merseyside (150), Strathclyde
(121), South Yorkshire (112), Tyne and Wear (110) and the West
Midlands (106). When variations in population are taken into
account, however, strong concentrations in two particular regions
can be noted. First, the North-East possesses four counties with
indices of over 2.10 — Northumberland (2.71), Tyne and Wear
(2.63) and Cleveland (2.57) all 'producing' professional footballers
at over two-and-a-half-times the national rate; and the coterminous
County Durham (2.13), which produces at over twice the national
norm. The second principal region of player production is the north-

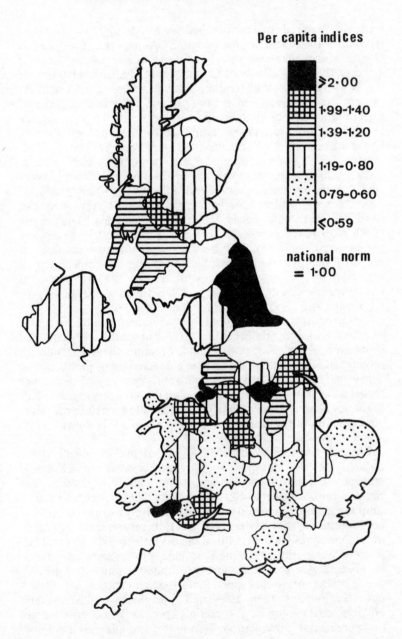

Fig. 4.10. *Per capita* 'production' of professional soccer players, 1979.

west, although only one county, Merseyside (2.70), has a *per capita* index more than twice the national norm. Adjoining Lancashire and Greater Manchester have high, but not spectacular, indices. In some respects, the Welsh county of Clwyd ought to be included as part of the North-West football region, since its index of 1.63 actually exceeds that of Greater Manchester (1.60). Individual counties of high production, but in no way part of any football region, include South Yorkshire which possesses an index of 2.41, and is quite unlike its neighbours, North Yorkshire (0.51) and West Yorkshire (0.96), and the South Wales county of West Glamorgan which, with an index of 2.45, is the main surprise of this analysis. Other surveys similar to the present one have revealed that South Wales 'produces' rather more professional footballers per head of its population than its rugby image would suggest.[25] Gwent (1.47) and South Glamorgan (1.90) contribute to make South Wales a soccer as well as a rugby region (see Chapter 6). Despite the intervening opportunities of playing for clubs in the Scottish League, central Scotland remains a major producer of English League footballers. The large county of Strathclyde, which includes Glasgow, has an index of 1.38, but the adjoining Central region has a high index of 1.76.

Low producers of professional footballers are, with the exception of North Yorkshire, almost entirely found in southern England and southern Scotland. A ring of counties around Greater London is revealed in Fig. 4.10 as being an area characterised by production at below half the national norm. The south-west is clearly another region which fails to produce professional footballers at above half the national rate. Greater detail on the absolute and relative producing capacities of the major and minor 'producers' is shown in Fig. 4.10 and Tables 4.1 and 4.2.

The counties ranked in Table 4.1 sound like a roll-call of the Industrial Revolution: today they are mainly in government development areas and unemployment is particularly high there. The counties ranked in Table 4.2, on the other hand, are either rural or southern in orientation and are mostly relatively prosperous. As has been traditional with professional sport, therefore, it can be argued that economic as much as cultural factors influence the regional differentiation in the production of élite professional sportsmen. Where employment opportunities are limited, a way out of the dole queue is via professional sport. Since the areas shown in Table 4.1 have traditionally been associated with heavy industry (shipbuilding, coal mining etc.), soccer also provided an alternative and more comfortable occupation, even in times of alternative employment. For this reason something of a tradition for the sport has evolved. Two exceptions seem to be West Yorkshire and Mid-

Table 4.1.   COUNTIES RANKING HIGH IN PER CAPITA
PRODUCTION OF FOOTBALLERS

| County | Per capita index | One player per | No. of players |
|--------|------------------|----------------|----------------|
| Northumberland | 2.71 | 10,372 | 28 |
| Merseyside | 2.70 | 10,411 | 150 |
| Tyne and Wear | 2.63 | 10,688 | 110 |
| Cleveland | 2.57 | 10,937 | 52 |
| West Glamorgan | 2.45 | 11,473 | 32 |
| South Yorkshire | 2.41 | 11,663 | 112 |
| Durham | 2.13 | 13,197 | 46 |
| South Glamorgan | 1.90 | 14,794 | 26 |
| Central Scotland | 1.76 | 15,971 | 17 |
| Clwyd | 1.63 | 17,245 | 22 |
| Greater Manchester | 1.60 | 17,568 | 152 |
| Staffordshire | 1.61 | 17,459 | 57 |
| Humberside | 1.50 | 18,739 | 45 |

*Source of original data:* Rollin (1979).

Table 4.2.   COUNTIES RANKING LOW ON PER CAPITA
PRODUCTION OF FOOTBALLERS

| County | Per capita index | One player per | No. of players |
|--------|------------------|----------------|----------------|
| Border | 0.00 | – | 0 |
| West Sussex | 0.09 | 312,322 | 2 |
| Dumfries/Galloway | 0.20 | 140,545 | 1 |
| Gloucester | 0.23 | 122,213 | 4 |
| Somerset | 0.27 | 104,107 | 4 |
| Cornwall | 0.27 | 104,107 | 4 |
| Hertfordshire | 0.30 | 93,697 | 10 |
| Kent | 0.35 | 80,312 | 18 |
| Suffolk | 0.38 | 73,971 | 8 |
| Berkshire | 0.42 | 66,926 | 10 |
| East Sussex | 0.43 | 65,370 | 10 |
| Surrey | 0.48 | 58,560 | 17 |
| Wiltshire | 0.49 | 57,365 | 9 |
| Grampian | 0.49 | 57,365 | 8 |

The sparsely-populated Scottish island groups of Orkney, Shetland and the Western
Isles, which between them produced no players, have been excluded.

*Source of original data:* see Table 4.1.

Glamorgan, where it is possible that the intervening opportunity of
rugby has diverted potential soccer players.

On the basis of the analysis of player production, a small number
of northern 'hotbeds' of soccer activity can be clearly identified. At
the same time it is worth noting that metropolitan counties generally

possess higher *per capita* indices than their hinterlands. London, for example, while possessing only a slightly above-average index, is twice as productive as the surrounding areas of very low emphasis. To a less marked extent, the same is true of Greater Birmingham (i.e. the West Midlands), Greater Manchester and Merseyside. The same is true of Glasgow and Belfast, though their significant contribution is understated because of the inclusion of many players of comparable standard who play in the Scottish League, and because of the aggregated nature of the areal units within which they are subsumed.

A final feature of the pattern of player production which is worthy of mention is the growing number of overseas-born players who have taken part in English football in recent years. The principal region of origin of immigrant footballers is the Caribbean. In 1972 only two Caribbean-born players were playing in the Football League; by 1980 the figure had risen to eleven. In 1979 the Football League lifted the ban on the importation of foreign players to British clubs, and the result has been a small movement of players from Argentina, the Netherlands, Yugoslavia and other nations.

## The movement of players

We have seen that the geography of player *production* exemplifies a strongly localised pattern. Professional clubs have the task of attracting players to a place which may be many kilometres from the players' homes. The *market* for professional footballers is 'the spatial arrangement of playing opportunities, or the points of consumption.'[26] This simple model, of production and consumption of footballers, is complicated by the hierarchical structure of the market — from the first to the ninety-second ranked club in the League. The larger and the more successful a club (Fig. 11), the larger its budget for spending on players, and hence the wider its geographical catchment for players. Prestigious clubs, wherever situated, are thus able to recruit from high *per capita* production areas while smaller clubs are restricted in their recruitment of initiate professionals to a more limited hinterland. The dramatic example shown in Fig. 4.11 is similar to the case of some of the larger, sports-oriented American universities out-recruiting the small state colleges.[27]

There are several ways of establishing the general pattern of movement of professional footballers. Konig considered the movement of players as revealed in the differences between their playing location in the early 1970s and their place of birth.[28] Such an analysis ignores the fact that footballers may return to their region of birth later, often at the end of their playing careers; it represents a 'snapshot', at

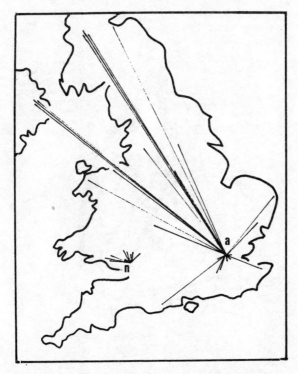

Fig. 4.11. Birthplaces of soccer players starting their professional careers with (a) Arsenal and (n) Newport County (1972 data base).

one moment in time, of a complex pattern of career movements which are going on continuously. Because there is a locational mismatch between the production and the consumption of players, some areas inevitably produce more players than they can consume locally. Fig. 4.12 identifies the main inter-regional migrations of players for those playing in the league in 1972: clearly, the main direction of flow is from the over-productive north (Fig. 4.10) to the deficient south. There is no reason to believe that the pattern has since changed in any significant way. The fact that the north is the smallest importer of players suggests that it satisfies most of its own demand. The south-east region, on the other hand (which in Fig. 4.12 includes East Anglia), imported over 25 per cent of all migrant players, the main flows coming from the north and Wales. Little out-migration of southern-born players appears to take place, suggesting some sort of southern bias in their perceptions. Indeed, if Fig. 4.12

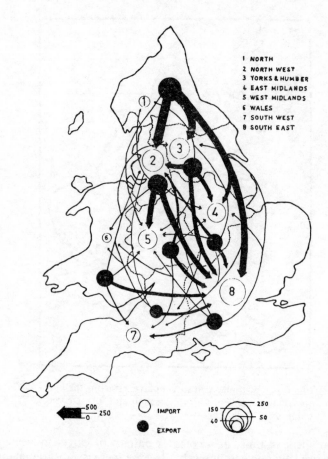

Fig. 4.12. The inter-regional migration of professional footballers (1972 data base — *source*: Konig 1972).

is typical, little northward movement at all takes place.

A more detailed case study of the migration pattern of players from one county may further elaborate the discussion. Durham is an example of a county which produces professional footballers at well above the national average rate, and in 1972 the largest importers of Durham-born talent were the West Riding of Yorkshire (14.3 per cent), Lancashire (12.8 per cent) and the North Riding (7.5 per cent). With only three League clubs in Durham itself, it is hardly surprising that it retained less than a quarter of the players it produced. The basic generalisation which can be drawn from the pattern shown in

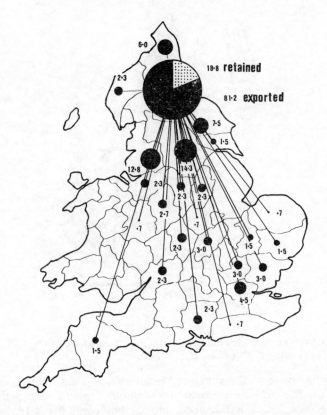

Fig. 4.13. Migration of soccer players from Durham. (1972 data base)
Figures refer to percentages of Durham-produced players (*source*: Konig
1972).

Fig. 4.13 is that as distance increases from the county of origin (in
this case, Durham), the number of players imported decreases. This
pattern of distance-decay has been found to exist for most other
counties,[29] and for the states of the U.S.A.[30]

A final approach to analysing player movement is to consider the
actual *transfer* of players between clubs over a given period. This
would exclude the large number of initial moves from non-league to
league clubs at the start of players' careers. If only inter-regional
moves are considered, 302 moves took place in the United Kingdom
between June 1975 and May 1977. This figure excludes temporary
transfers and 109 intra-regional moves, over 36 per cent of which
were within south-east England. Hence, almost three times as many

Fig. 4.14. The dominant interregional flows of transferred soccer players, June 1975–May 1977 (*source*: Bale 1979*a*).

transfers of footballers involved inter-regional than intra-regional moves. The 302 inter-regional moves would display a very jumbled and complex pattern if mapped, and for that reason Fig. 4.14 shows the *dominant* flows, using a technique called the Nystuen-Dacey method (described in Appendix A). Essentially, this technique generalises the complex pattern of lines which would emerge from the mapping of individual inter-club transfers. Fig. 4.14 reveals that for the two-year period, the dominant flows of transferred players were towards the south of the country. The south-east of England is confirmed as the magnet for transferred players from several other regions. The West Midlands is a minor focus, while the north-west and Yorkshire/Humberside are independent regions; in other words, they have larger inflows of transferred players than outflows.

This short-term pattern mirrors the long-term trend shown in Fig. 4.12. A nodal structure of football regions based on inter-regional flows of transferred players with hierarchical movement being dominant can be identified. The possibility that such flows represent some kind of upward social mobility in the hierarchy of football clubs is no more than speculation, but it cannot be entirely ignored.

Professional football, Britain's major sport in terms of spectator involvement and media coverage, possesses locational characteristics which were moulded over 100 years ago with the development of professionalism and subsequently the formation of the League in the north of England. Locational inertia has resulted in a pattern at the present time that fails to mirror regional variations in employment; a reduction of spatial competition among clubs would almost certainly benefit the clubs concerned. However, because football is not run with profit maximisation in mind, it is not surprising that a less than ideal location pattern is the result. Nonetheless, this chapter has suggested that there are, almost inexorably, signs of increasing rationality in the geography of the industry as a whole. The thinning out of the lower end of regional football hierarchies, the replacing of clubs at the economic periphery of the country by those at the 'centre', and the latent suburbanisation of football all illustrate this trend.

But in broad terms its 'northernness' seems to be a continuing characteristic. More clubs and more footballers (per head of the population) are found north of the river Trent. The dominant flows of migrant footballers are from north to south, and our mental map of football to some extent reflects the reality. Scotland has been underemphasised and almost certainly deserves credit for being one of Britain's football hotbeds; Allen records that *family* outings to football matches are twice as popular there, per head of the population, as they are in England.[31] Also, in 1974 we know that 26 per cent of the adult population in Scotland paid to watch soccer.[32]

This chapter has focused on football as a spectator sport. It remains to be seen in the next chapter whether the geographical characteristics of recreational football mirror in any way the geography of the professional game.

## REFERENCES

1. Magoun (1929).
2. Dunning (1971).
3. Magoun (1931).
4. Dunning (1971), Walvin (1975), Young (1971), Marples (1954), Magoun (1938).
5. Pickford (1941).
6. Mason (1980).
7. Mason (1980).
8. Allison (1978), Taylor (1976).
9. Clarke and Jefferson (1976).
10. Mason (1980); see also Baker (1980).
11. For a review of the economics of football, see Sloane (1980).
12. Douglas (1974).

13. Department of Education and Science (1968).
14. Rivett (1975).
15. Department of Education and Science (1968).
16. Wiseman (1977).
17. Sloane (1971).
18. *Economist* (1965).
19. Bale and Gowing (1976).
20. E.g., see Quirk (1973).
21. E.g. Critcher (1979).
22. Political and Economic Planning (1951).
23. Rivett (1975).
24. Rollin (1979).
25. See Konig (1972), Bale (1978*a*) and Gavin (1979).
26. Rooney (1974).
27. Rooney (1974).
28. Konig (1972).
29. See Konig (1972).
30. Allen (1968).
31. I.P.C. (1975).
32. Allen (1968).

# 5

# FOOTBALL AS A RECREATIONAL SPORT

Although professional football receives more media coverage, it is the recreational game which outdoes all other British sports in numbers of participants. It is impossible to know the exact number of active footballers. According to the Central Statistical Office's publication *Social Trends*, 20 per cent of the male population aged between sixteen and twenty-four engage actively in football.[1] Estimates of between 780,000 and 1,170,000 have been made for the actual numbers involved, and it is likely that, in addition, about 6,000 women now play the sport. This chapter considers recreational football from three main perspectives: first, the regional differences in the adoption of the game, as measured by the number of clubs per county; secondly, regional differences in the provision of pitches; and thirdly, the geography of the rapidly emerging sport of women's football.

## Patterns of club location

Although the professional game is in decline, both as a profession and measured by the number of spectators who annually watch the sport, recreational football is growing in popularity. In 1948 the number of clubs affiliated to the Football Association totalled 17,973; by 1966 it had risen to 25,217 and by 1979 to 39,079.[2] From data made available by the Football Association and the Welsh F.A., an absolute and *per capita* analysis of the geography of recreational football is possible. Strictly, this represents a geography of opportunity since it is based on the number of clubs, but it seems likely that the number of clubs per county is strongly and positively correlated with number of players per county,[3] in which case the analysis may approximate to a geography of emphasis as well.

In absolute terms the counties of Lancashire (4,588 clubs or 11.3 per cent of the total), Greater London (4,160 or 10.6 per cent), Warwickshire (2,776 or 6.8 per cent) and the West Riding of Yorkshire (2,763 or 6.8 per cent) are the main centres, and together account for over 35 per cent of all clubs. While some northern counties are important foci of recreational football, the large number of southern counties shown in Table 5.1 suggests that recreational soccer may not mirror the geographical pattern of the professional game described in the previous chapter. Indeed, the data in Table 5.1

Table 5.1.   ABSOLUTE NUMBER OF FOOTBALL CLUBS
IN ENGLAND AND WALES, 1979
(*top twenty counties, pre-1974 boundaries*)

| County | No. of clubs | % |
|---|---|---|
| Lancashire | 4,588 | 11.3 |
| Greater London | 4,160 | 10.2 |
| West Riding | 2,793 | 6.8 |
| Warwick (including Birmingham) | 2,776 | 6.8 |
| Essex | 1,930 | 4.7 |
| Kent | 1,524 | 3.7 |
| Cheshire | 1,268 | 3.1 |
| Surrey | 1,268 | 3.1 |
| Durham | 1,250 | 3.1 |
| Berks and Bucks | 1,119 | 2.7 |
| Sussex | 1,058 | 2.6 |
| Stafford | 1,032 | 2.5 |
| Derby | 917 | 2.2 |
| Nottingham | 846 | 2.1 |
| Lincoln | 821 | 2.0 |
| Hertford | 796 | 1.9 |
| Leicester and Rutland | 742 | 1.8 |
| Gloucester | 731 | 1.8 |
| Somerset | 674 | 1.6 |
| Glamorgan | 634 | 1.5 |

*Source:* unpublished statistics, Football Association, Welsh F.A., 1979.

reveal that over a quarter of all football clubs in England and Wales are found in Greater London and neighbouring counties.

The 40,722 clubs in England and Wales represent one club per 1,193 people, and this we will represent as an index of 1.00 against which the county indices can be compared. *Per capita* leaders are hardly northern in character or location. In England, the only county with over twice the national norm is Lincolnshire (index of 2.08). Anecdotal evidence suggests that the area around Grimsby in particular is 'football-mad',[4] a view supported by the evidence presented here. Lincolnshire is followed by Northamptonshire (1.70), Essex (1.70), Cornwall and Surrey (both 1.51), the English counties with more than one-and-a-half times the national norm. It should be noted, however, that in Wales the rural county of Powys is a surprisingly high *per capita* provider of football clubs (index of 1.82).

Consideration of Fig. 5.1 and Table 5.2 reveals that the geography of recreational football is considerably different from that of the professional game. It is clearly simplistic to describe football *per se* as a northern sport. The top twenty counties in Table 5.2 include only three which are strictly northern in orientation. Fig. 5.1 reveals a high level of recreational football activity in two suburban-rural

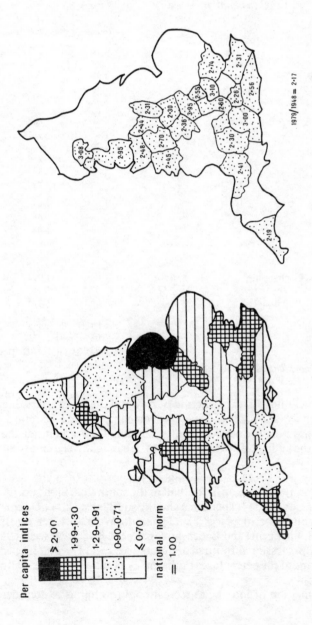

Fig. 5.1 (*left*). *Per capita* emphasis on recreational soccer, 1979 (*source of original data*: see Table 5.1). Fig. 5.2 (*right*). Counties in which the rate of growth in the number of soccer clubs, 1948—79, was greater than the national growth rate (*source of original data*: see Table 5.1).

Table 5.2.   PER CAPITA PROVISION OF FOOTBALL CLUBS:
COUNTIES WITH ABOVE AVERAGE PER CAPITA INDICES,
ENGLAND AND WALES, 1979
(*English counties — pre-1974 boundaries*)

| County | Index | One club per |
|---|---|---|
| Lincolnshire | 2.08 | 573 |
| Powys | 1.82 | 655 |
| Northamptonshire | 1.70 | 702 |
| Essex | 1.70 | 702 |
| Surrey | 1.51 | 790 |
| Cornwall | 1.51 | 790 |
| Herefordshire | 1.42 | 840 |
| Westmorland | 1.31 | 911 |
| Kent | 1.30 | 918 |
| Norfolk | 1.28 | 930 |
| Suffolk | 1.27 | 939 |
| Gwynedd | 1.26 | 947 |
| Derbyshire | 1.24 | 962 |
| Bedfordshire | 1.22 | 978 |
| Somerset | 1.18 | 1,011 |
| Hampshire | 1.14 | 1,046 |
| Shropshire | 1.12 | 1,065 |
| Leicester/Rutland | 1.11 | 1,077 |
| Wiltshire | 1.11 | 1,077 |
| Berkshire/Buckinghamshire | 1.09 | 1,094 |
| Lancashire | 1.07 | 1,114 |
| Durham | 1.06 | 1,125 |
| Oxfordshire | 1.04 | 1,147 |
| Nottinghamshire | 1.03 | 1,158 |
| Hertfordshire | 1.03 | 1,158 |
| Sussex | 1.02 | 1,170 |

*Source of original data:* see Table 5.1.

arcs, one including Essex, Kent and Surrey and the other consisting of a broken arc made up of Lincoln, Northampton and Hereford-Powys. Within the former lies Greater London (0.67) and inside the latter are the industrial Midlands, both areas relatively empty of soccer activity.

Evidence also suggests that a higher proportion of males aged 11 – 40 actually participate in football in the south than in the north. Figures for London (13.4 per cent) and the south-east (11.1 per cent) contrast with those of places like Tyne and Wear (6.1 per cent), Durham (8.4 per cent) and Lancashire (6.2 per cent). Such seedbeds of modern professional football are more like rural Devon (6.7 per cent) in terms of the percentages of the male population who actually play the game.

A final method of looking at recreational football is to consider regional differences in the growth of the game since the Second World War, as measured by the changing number of clubs. The 1979 total of 39,079 football clubs in England is 2.17 times greater than the number in 1948. This national multiplier can be compared with the multipliers for individual counties to identify regional differences in the rate of growth of the game. The most spectacular growth rates have been in Northamptonshire, Westmorland and Hampshire, each of which has more than three times as many football clubs as in 1948. The *general* pattern, however, as shown in Fig. 5.2, is one where counties with the highest growth rates being mainly located south of the Mersey-Humber axis. North of this line only two counties possess higher growth rates than the average for the country as a whole, while south of the Severn-Thames axis only two counties do not possess them.

It is clear, therefore, that to call football a northern sport is a gross over-simplification. Recreational football is in fact mainly associated with rural and suburban England, although this is not to say that there are no rural counties with low indices (e.g. Devon and Cumbria).

## Football in the north: an intra-regional approach

The variation in *per capita* emphasis and opportunity for recreational football within one region can be exemplified by reference to the northern region. This case-study illustrates how some of the patterns described in the previous section referring to the national level are reproduced at the regional level.[5]

Within the northern region (Fig. 5.3), recreational football is concentrated in an absolute sense in the major cities of Sunderland (272 clubs), Newcastle (210), Gateshead (152), Carlisle (122) and Stockton-on-Tees (122). In *per capita* terms, however, a number of areas possess indices of emphasis greater than those of the towns of the north-east coast. Only two of these towns have indices above one-and-a-quarter times the regional norm, namely Sunderland (1.28) and Hartlepool (1.43). The remainder of the industrial north-east has below-average or average provision of clubs. In fact, the major area of emphasis, when measured by the number of clubs per head, is found far away from the traditional areas of heavy industry. Carlisle (1.87) and Derwentside (1.84) possess almost twice as many clubs as the regional norm (Fig. 5.4).

The proportion of footballers per head of the regional population is one per 59 (index of 1.00). In absolute terms Newcastle is the regional leader with over 4,000 active players, but in *per capita* terms Hartlepool (1.39) and Sunderland (1.29) are again dominant. Away

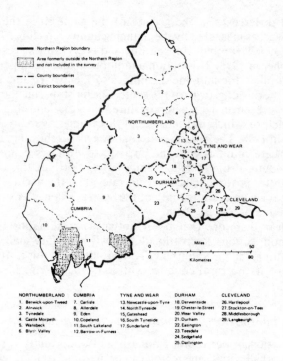

| NORTHUMBERLAND | CUMBRIA | TYNE AND WEAR | DURHAM | CLEVELAND |
|---|---|---|---|---|
| 1. Berwick-upon-Tweed | 7. Carlisle | 13. Newcastle-upon-Tyne | 18. Derwentside | 26. Hartlepool |
| 2. Alnwick | 8. Allerdale | 14. North Tyneside | 19. Chester-le-Street | 27. Stockton-on-Tees |
| 3. Tynedale | 9. Eden | 15. Gateshead | 20. Wear Valley | 28. Middlesborough |
| 4. Castle Morpeth | 10. Copeland | 16. South Tyneside | 21. Durham | 29. Langbaurgh |
| 5. Wansbeck | 11. South Lakeland | 17. Sunderland | 22. Easington | |
| 6. Blyth Valley | 12. Barrow-in-Furness | | 23. Teesdale | |
| | | | 24. Sedgefield | |
| | | | 25. Darlington | |

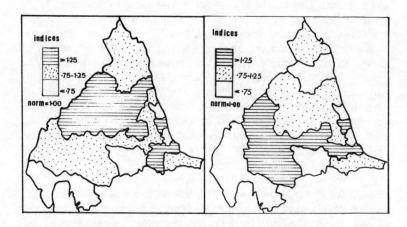

Fig. 5.3 (*top*). Sub-divisions of the northern region (*source*: Horn 1975).
Fig. 5.4 (*below, left*). The northern region — *per capita* analysis of soccer clubs. Fig. 5.5 (*below, right*). The northern region — *per capita* analysis of number of soccer participants.

from the north-east coast, Carlisle and Derwentside (1.72 and 1.68) both emphasise recreational football at over one-and-a-half times the regional norm.

Fig. 5.5 reveals that recreational football is not a feature of the urban centres of the north-east. North and South Tyneside, in particular have very low indices (0.56 and 0.70 respectively), reflecting the poor provision of football facilities in the inner cities — a fact that can be broadly applied to the entire country. In Tyne and Wear, for example, pitch provision is one per 3,329, but in South Tyneside it is only one per 3,935. These kinds of comparisons could be made for many other regions. For example, in East Anglia Norwich has one pitch per 1,600 while Great Yarmouth has one per 4,030. However, perhaps one of the starkest contrasts is between inner city and suburb. In London, the borough of Southwark has one pitch for every 6,317 people, while more suburban Greenwich has one per 1,497.[6] Such deprivation is merely typical of Britain's inner cities.

## Women's football[7]

Although women's football has been played in Britain sporadically and informally for several decades, its formal organisation for British women dates from 1969, when the Women's Football Association was formed. It seems likely that the exclusion of women from football had been largely culturally determined and that only with the changing self-perception of women and their role in society did football became a serious sport for both sexes.

The sport has grown very rapidly in recent years. In 1969, only fifty-one clubs were registered as initial members of the WFA, but by 1979 the number had grown to 278, with twenty-one leagues organised regionally. Today it can be conservatively estimated that about 5,000 women participate regularly in football in England and Wales. It is anticipated that the numbers of players and of clubs will continue to increase for some time to come.

The geographical pattern of women's football displays quite marked regional differences. In an absolute sense the south-east of England has the largest number of clubs, 105 or 37.8 per cent of the total. Somewhat surprisingly, this is followed by the south-west with forty-five clubs (16.2 per cent). No other Standard Region has over 15 per cent of the total number of clubs. The more meaningful *per capita* analysis reveals women's football as a dominantly southern phenomenon. The national norm of one club per 177,000 people (index of 1.00) needs to be compared with the situation in south-west England where one club is found for every 95,000 (index of 1.86) and

East Anglia where there is one for every 130,000 (index of 1.36). Within these two regions, certain individual counties have very high *per capita* indices. Devon has 4.57 times the national average number of clubs per head of the population, while the index for Cornwall is 3.11. In East Anglia, Norfolk and Suffolk have indices of 1.63 and 1.56 respectively. The south-east of England, while having an overall regional index of 1.10, contains six counties with indices of over 1.30 — Kent (2.84) and Bedfordshire (2.19) being the main foci (Table 5.3).

The north of England generally underemphasises the women's game. It is true that together the counties of the north-west have an average index of 1.06 and that Cheshire has a very high *per capita* figure of 2.35, but the North and Yorkshire — Humberside have indices of only 0.51 and 0.40 respectively. Even lower indices are found for the conurbations within these regions. The most dramatic example is West Yorkshire with an index of 0.17. Clear evidence of the north-south dichotomy is shown in Fig. 5.6.

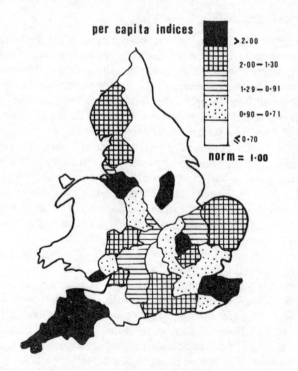

Fig. 5.6. Women's soccer — *per capita* playing opportunity (*source*: Bale, 1980*b*).

Table 5.3. WOMEN'S FOOTBALL IN ENGLAND AND WALES:
COUNTIES RANKING HIGH ON PER CAPITA
PROVISION OF CLUBS, 1979

|  | Per capita index | One club per 1,000 | No. of clubs |
|---|---|---|---|
| Devon | 4.57 | 39 | 24 |
| Cornwall | 3.11 | 57 | 7 |
| Kent | 2.84 | 62 | 23 |
| Cheshire | 2.35 | 75 | 12 |
| South Glamorgan | 2.26 | 78 | 5 |
| Bedfordshire | 2.19 | 81 | 6 |
| Nottingham | 2.16 | 82 | 12 |
| Norfolk | 1.63 | 108 | 6 |
| Suffolk | 1.56 | 113 | 5 |
| Lancashire | 1.55 | 114 | 12 |
| Worcester/Hereford | 1.51 | 117 | 5 |
| Cumbria | 1.49 | 119 | 4 |
| West Sussex | 1.44 | 123 | 5 |
| Hampshire | 1.36 | 130 | 11 |
| Avon | 1.35 | 131 | 7 |
| Berkshire | 1.35 | 131 | 5 |
| Hertfordshire | 1.31 | 134 | 7 |

*Source:* Bale 1980*b*.

Broadly, therefore, women's football is a southern sport. Of the seventeen counties with indices of more than 1.30, eleven lie south of a line joining the Severn estuary and The Wash. Of the remaining counties, Hereford/Worcester, Cheshire and Cumbria are relatively high-status 'suburban' counties. The relative absence of women's football in the *industrial* north might be attributed to the more rigid cultural barriers against its adoption. As we have seen, the north has been traditionally associated with men's football; within such a working-class regional culture, where sex roles are rigidly demarcated, women may find it more difficult to find acceptance in participation in soccer.

Women's soccer is also something of a rural activity; of the conurbations, only Merseyside (1.10) has an index of more than 1.00. It is also overwhelmingly a small town sport. The rural-urban dichotomy is strikingly similar to that observed by Rooney who, for a variety of women's sports in the United States, noted that large-city girls tend to be conditioned away from sport because of the large number of intervening leisure activities which exist. In rural areas, on the other hand, fewer such opportunities exist, and sport is seen as an acceptable social activity for girls.[8] These, however, are inevitably generalisations, and exceptions will readily be found in Fig. 5.6. The precise nature of the barriers to the more widespread adoption of women's soccer have yet to be thoroughly researched.

Unlike professional football, the recreational sport is continuing to grow in the last quarter of the twentieth century, for both men and women. Regions associated with the professional game are not also especially associated with the recreational version. However, the relative absence of many very high or many very low per capita indices shows not only that the men's game is widespread throughout the country but also that the degree of localisation of recreational football is limited. In England only one county has an index of more than 2.00 and two have indices of less than 0.65. Above average rates of growth of the national sport are, however, concentrated in the south and Midlands.

Women's football is a relatively recent innovation. It in no way mirrors the stereotype image of northern, working-class football. However, what is clear is that quite marked regional differences exist in the rate of growth, and the attitudes towards women's football. Of especial importance for both men and women is the relative neglect of the conurbations and inner cities in terms of club and pitch provision. Dual use of school facilities might go some way towards solving the problem of under-provision of pitches and continued development of synthetic surfaces (e.g. 'Astroturf') can also be expected.

## REFERENCES

1. Central Statistical Office (1979).
2. Football Association (1979), unpublished data.
3. Horn (1975).
4. Cunningham (1980).
5. Horn (1975).
6. Bale (1979a).
7. For a more detailed examination of women's football see Bale (1980b).
8. Rooney (1974).

# 6

## RUGBY: A DIVIDED SPORT

Two types of rugby are found in Britain. The union game differs from rugby league, not only (to a minor extent) in the rules and the number of players per side, but perhaps more significantly in its location pattern. Although rugby union is played throughout the country, marked localisation is found. But in rugby league, the localisation is dramatic. Dunning and Sheard, the principal academic chroniclers of the sport, summarise the social and geographical pattern thus: 'rugby union is played throughout the British Isles, primarily by members of the middle classes, whereas rugby league is restricted almost solely to the counties of Yorkshire and Lancashire. It also recruits its personnel, players and spectators, though not to the same extent its administrative staff, mainly from the working class.'[1]

Rugby league, in particular, possesses strong regional connotations. Certain towns are identified almost immediately with the sport (Fig. 6.1). The playwright, Colin Welland, has written: 'In southwest Lancashire, babes don't toddle; they sidestep. Queueing women talk about 'nipping round the blindside'. Rugby league provides our cultural adrenalin. It's a physical manifestation of our rules of life, comradeship, honest endeavour, and a staunch, often ponderous allegiance to fair play.'[2]

*Sporting Towns of the North : 1. St. Helens*

Fig. 6.1. St. Helens: sport evokes urban images (*source*: *The Sunday Times Magazine*, 13 March 1978).

Rugby union is also identified with particular places. 'Wales is known as the "land of rugby". For many a Welshman, to like soccer or any other game is positively un-Welsh.'[3] An attempt to make an objective measurement of the subjective association between rugby union and Wales was undertaken using the method described on page 17. Fig. 6.2 strongly confirms Wales as having a strong rugby image. Of the respondents to the mental mapping test 40 per cent included Wales within their 'rugby region'. Over 70 per cent identified rugby union with South Wales in particular and over 80 per cent with South-East Wales. To a less degree (30 per cent of the respondents), the adjoining English counties (e.g. Gloucester) and those of Southern Scotland also possess something of a rugby image.

Such regional sports images demand empirical verification or rejection — which is one of the purposes of the present chapter. In addition, the chapter focuses on three particular aspects of rugby: first, the bifurcation of rugby league and rugby union is described; secondly, the present-day geography of rugby league, both professional and amateur, is identified; and thirdly, the different degrees of localisation of rugby union are described.

## The geography of schism[4]

Because the games are essentially the same, there has been a constant flow of players from union to league teams. Fig. 6.3 indicates the migration paths of those union players who joined league clubs in 1979. Movement from league to union clubs is, however, expressly forbidden by the union administration. This is because rugby league is overtly professional whereas the union game retains — superficially, at least — the amateur ethos of the nineteenth-century sporting gentleman. This dichotomy between professional and amateur led to the parting of the ways between the two rugby codes. The story takes us back to the late nineteenth century.

Dunning and Sheard suggest that in the 1890s when the rift between the northern rugby professionals and the southern amateurs was at its most serious, a growing breakdown was occurring in English class relationships. Whereas professionalism in soccer had come 'towards the end of a 30-year period of relatively harmonious relations between social classes,'[5] professionalism in rugby was taking place at a time of mounting class conflict. As a result, the 'Simon Pure' amateurs of the (southern) rugby union resisted professionalism in rugby much more strongly than they had in soccer. Indeed, rugby union came to replace soccer as the 'gentleman's sport'. Hence, argue Dunning and Sheard, it was in rugby that the social strains of British society in the late nineteenth century led to

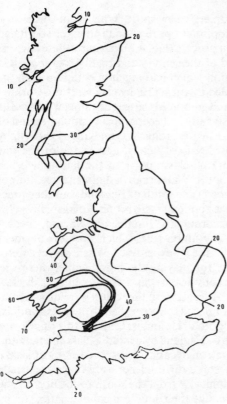

Fig. 6.2. A mental map of Britain's rugby union regions. The isolines represent the degree to which respondents identified different parts of the country with rugby union (figs. refer to percentages).

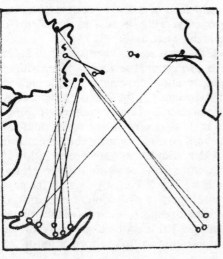

Fig. 6.3. Transfers of players from rugby union to rugby league clubs, 1979. Apart from three intra-regional moves, all migrations were from either South Wales or Greater London (*source of data*: *The Observer*, 3 February 1980).

the development of a completely new sport. Whereas in soccer, the cultural barriers to the adoption of professionalism in the south had *slowed down* the diffusion process (Fig. 4.2), in rugby these barriers had intensified by the end of the century and totally *prevented* it.

South Wales was a region which had much in common with the north of England, but failed to attract rugby league. If the working class in the north of England embraced the league game, why was the same not the case for the socially and economically similar region of South Wales? Today South Wales is almost synonymous with rugby union, a subject which is discussed below, and is one of the few regions where it is a working-class sport. In the late nineteenth century it seems that the South Wales rugby administrators did not adhere to the amateur ethos of the south of England; but they prac- ticed a conspiracy of silence about *de facto* professionalism in Welsh rugby. Clubs in Wales, according to Dunning and Sheard, 'persis- tently disregarded the rugby union rules which prohibit payment of money in excess of "limited" expenses.'[6] When players were, in effect, receiving money for playing the union game, there was no incentive to develop rugby league, and as we will see, the few attempts to introduce rugby league into the region were disasters.

The handling game, as opposed to soccer, had formed its adminis- trative body, the Rugby Football Union, in 1891. At this time it was played mainly in the south of England by a middle-class clientele and run by 'gentlemen' who strongly upheld a sport-for-sport's-sake philosophy, but it had become diffused not only down the social hierarchy but also geographically from the south to the north. The northern rugby clubs were, like their southern counterparts, run by gentlemen; but they were gentlemen of a lower social status. The northern clubs were more open socially because in the northern towns barriers to social interaction were lower.

Just as professionalism was taking place in soccer (see Fig. 4.2), so too attempts were made to professionalise rugby by providing players with payments as compensation for wages lost while playing rugby. By 1886, however, it was decided by the R.F.U. to enact rules to stop the incipient professionalisation of rugby in the north, espe- cially Yorkshire. However, in 1893 the Yorkshire representatives proposed to the R.F.U. that 'broken time' payments be legitimised. These payments were being widely adopted, as were the formation of leagues with a system of relegation and promotion. However, the southern amateurs who dominated the R.F.U. argued that the pay- ments detracted from the 'pure' sporting philosophy which formed the basis of recreational-participatory sport. Not surprisingly, there- fore, there was no way that the R.F.U. would give way to the northern requests and this opposition led to the formation of the

Northern Rugby Football Union in 1895. Yorkshire clubs were joined in this venture by a number of clubs from Lancashire and Cheshire, and by the end of the century professionalism had become a central feature of the new-formed rugby league.

Several geographical questions arise from this brief summary of the events leading up to the bifurcation in rugby. Why did professional rugby fail to diffuse itself to the south of England when professional soccer had succeeded? Why did other working-class areas, notably South Wales, fail to embrace professional rugby? What was so particular about the north which produced such a localised pattern of sporting activity as now exists (see below)? Rugby league could not gain a footing among the working class outside the north because soccer was already entrenched as the working-class spectator sport. In addition, its cloth-cap image and its professionalism meant that it could not compete seriously with rugby union as a middle-class sport. So it was destined almost from the start, to be a regionally limited, minority sport. We will now consider the extent to which it remains geographically limited.

## The localisation of rugby league[7]

Rugby league is one of the most regionally concentrated sports in Britain. Thirty professional clubs form the pinnacle, and their location is shown in Fig. 6.4. The dominant counties are West Yorkshire and Greater Manchester, which accommodate eighteen (60 per cent) of the total number of clubs. Minor concentrations of clubs are also found in Cumbria, Cheshire and Merseyside. The professional game is organised in two leagues, teams being promoted and relegated as in soccer.

Attempts to introduce rugby league into other parts of the country have been mainly abortive. For example, in the late 1900s a small concentration of clubs existed in South Wales (at Ebbw Vale, Merthyr Tydfil, Barry, Aberdare, mid-Rhondda and Treherbert). Between the world wars, there was an attempt to introduce rugby league into the industrial north-east, again with very limited success. The game was even introduced temporarily into the metropolis. It was suggested that a declining northern team, Wigan Highfield, should become London Highfield and play at White City Stadium in order to boost the stadium's attractiveness. The gamble failed because of apathy and mounting costs, and the players and officials re-migrated north to become Liverpool Stanley. Subsequently, sports entrepreneurs in the south-east launched two London clubs, Acton and Willesden and Streatham and Mitcham, but within a year of their formation both teams had failed through lack of interest and

Fig. 6.4. The present and former location of professional rugby league. The spatial margins to viability of this sport have contracted over time.

consequent insolvency. Other temporary outposts of rugby league are shown in Fig. 6.4 which reveals that the present pattern of spatial organisation of the professional game represents the result of a spatial contraction or retrenchment of sports activity — a process known to some geographers as paracme.[8] In 1980 the league game was reintroduced to London when Fulham Football Club diversified its activities and set up a rugby league team. In 1981 it was announced that Carlisle and Cardiff soccer clubs had done the same. Time will tell how successful these ventures will be.

## Amateur rugby league

'Before the advent of the British Amateur Rugby League Association in 1973 amateur rugby league, though still vigorous in schools, was in general in a chronic state, disorganised, ill-disciplined, dying. In less than five years a remarkable change has been wrought. A flourishing sport is now played by at least 80,000 amateurs, schoolboys and students.'[9] The amateur game is played in twenty-eight local leagues. However, Table 6.1 and Fig. 6.5 reveal that the amateur game is still dominantly northern. In the number of its amateur clubs, West Yorkshire is both the absolute and *per capita* leader, possessing 45.7 per cent of the total of national senior clubs and a *per capita* index of 11.99, representing one club per 16,000 of its population compared with the national norm of one per 192,000. Other spectacularly high *per capita* indices are found in Humberside (9.80) and Cumbria, which though only having 6.4 per cent of the clubs has a *per capita* index of 7.31. The amateur game has so far failed to penetrate the north-east, traditionally a bastion of soccer.

Two caveats need to be applied to Table 6.1 and Fig. 6.5. Oxford, with an index of 0.36, is shown solely as a result of the adoption of rugby league at the University. While this does not provide the opportunity for participation by local residents outside the University, it nevertheless reflects the growth of the sport in one of the traditional seats of the establishment. In addition, the growth of the sport among youth in Scotland, notably around Edinburgh, is not shown on the map, which refers only to senior participation.

Geographically, amateur rugby league differs in one significant way from the professional game. Whereas the spatial margins to viability of the professional version have (until very recently) been progressively contracting, those for the amateur game have been expanding, albeit at a rather modest rate. It seems likely that amateur rugby league will continue to grow and attract converts from the union game, which may for some be less attractive to play.

Table 6.1.   AMATEUR RUGBY LEAGUE: OPPORTUNITIES FOR
PARTICIPATION, 1979

| County | No. of clubs | | Per capita index | One club per |
|--------|------|------|------|------|
| | No. | % | | |
| West Yorkshire | 129 | 45.7 | 11.99 | 16,066 |
| Humberside | 43 | 15.2 | 9.80 | 19,660 |
| Greater Manchester | 33 | 11.7 | 2.38 | 81,054 |
| Cheshire | 19 | 6.7 | 4.00 | 72,005 |
| Cumbria | 18 | 6.4 | 7.31 | 26,350 |
| South Yorkshire | 11 | 3.9 | 1.62 | 118,545 |
| North Yorkshire | 10 | 3.5 | 2.94 | 65,400 |
| Merseyside | 10 | 3.5 | 1.23 | 156,180 |
| Lancashire | 4 | 1.4 | 0.56 | 342,025 |
| London | 3 | 1.1 | 0.08 | 2,323,367 |
| Oxford | 1 | 0.3 | 0.36 | 539,400 |
| West Midlands | 1 | 0.3 | 0.07 | 2,729,900 |
| Great Britain | 282 | 100.0 | 1.00 | 192,607 |

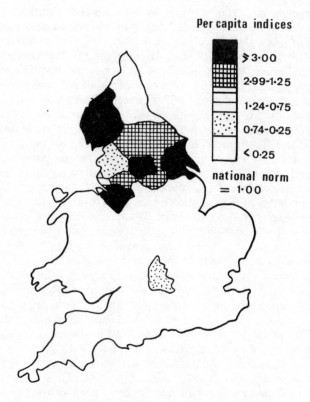

Per capita indices

≥3·00

2·99–1·25

1·24–0·75

0·74–0·25

<0·25

national norm
= 1·00

Fig. 6.5. Amateur rugby league: *per capita* playing opportunity, 1979 (*source of data*: British Amateur Rugby League, 1979).

The extreme form of localisation in rugby league can be interpreted as an important element of northern culture. The *facts* of the geography of the League game fit the image (Fig. 6.1) quite well; it *is* a northern sport. The extent to which the regional sports stereotype accorded to rugby union fits the reality is the subject of the next section.

## The location of rugby union

In contrast to rugby league, rugby union is played throughout Britain but is, as we have seen, popularly associated with particular regions, notably Wales. Also in contrast to the league game, the union code had spread to a large number of countries throughout the world, Thaman suggesting that by 1973 no fewer than fifty-nine countries had played rugby at some time.[10] In Britain a total of 2,054 rugby union clubs exist. In absolute terms, Greater London is the main centre with 178 clubs or 8.7 per cent of the total. However, the significance of South Wales is confirmed by the fact that the counties of Gwent (98 clubs or 4.8 per cent) and Dyfed (82 or 4.0 per cent) are ranked second and third in absolute terms. The Scottish county of Strathclyde (74 clubs or 3.6 per cent) and another Welsh county, South Glamorgan (70 or 3.4 per cent) complete the counties with seventy or more clubs.

The 2,054 rugby union clubs in Britain represent one club per 26,440 of the population — the national norm which can be represented as an index of 1.00 for purposes of comparison with individual counties. Table 6.2 shows the counties which emphasise rugby union at over one-and-a-third times the national rate. The regional rugby stereotype, South Wales, provides five out of the top seven counties with a mid-Wales and Scottish border county making up the other two areas. The South Wales counties possess very high *per capita* indices. Dyfed — possessing a hotbed of rugby in the Llanelli area — has over six-and-a-half times the number of rugby clubs per head of the population than the country as a whole. Gwent has an index of 5.90, West and South Glamorgan around 4.80 each and mid-Glamorgan 3.33. The more rural county of Powys also has a high index (3.51). In England the main focus of rugby union is undeniably the south-west. Cornwall (index of 2.94), Gloucestershire (2.74), Devon (1.48) and Avon (1.73) have higher indices than any other English county outside the south-west. The proximity of this part of England to South Wales helps to explain the high degree of localisation of rugby in the latter region.

Smith and Williams, in their scholarly history of Welsh rugby,[11] relate how football, having been introduced into Wales in the same way as elsewhere (i.e. by the products of Oxford and Cambridge and the private schools), developed a bias towards rugby in the south and soccer in the north. It seems that in South Wales the relative significance of rugby resulted from three factors. First, South Wales is contiguous with the west of England where the rural counties of Hereford, Gloucester, Somerset and Devon were strongholds of the rugby game, soccer being associated rather with the urban-industrial environment. In the 1870s and 1880s, Welsh clubs needed fixtures outside the local area in order to improve their game. As Smith and Williams comment, 'the twin considerations of communications and travel costs dictated that those fixtures would be with the nearest England had to offer'.[12]

Table 6.2*a*.   COUNTIES WITH A STRONG EMPHASIS
ON RUGBY UNION

| County | Index | One club per | No. of clubs |
|---|---|---|---|
| Dyfed | 6.67 | 3,964 | 82 |
| Border | 6.58 | 4,019 | 25 |
| Gwent | 5.90 | 4,482 | 98 |
| West Glamorgan | 4.82 | 5,486 | 67 |
| South Glamorgan | 4.80 | 5,509 | 70 |
| Powys | 3.51 | 7,534 | 14 |
| Mid-Glamorgan | 3.33 | 7,941 | 68 |
| Cornwall | 2.94 | 8,994 | 46 |
| Gloucestershire | 2.74 | 9,651 | 51 |
| Islands | 1.94 | 13,640 | 5 |
| Gwynedd | 1.86 | 14,219 | 16 |
| Lothian | 1.75 | 15,110 | 50 |
| Avon | 1.73 | 15,285 | 60 |
| Devon | 1.48 | 17,867 | 33 |
| Warwickshire | 1.47 | 17,988 | 26 |
| Highlands | 1.39 | 19,024 | 10 |
| Surrey | 1.38 | 19,162 | 52 |
| Cumbria | 1.34 | 19,734 | 24 |

Table 6.2*b*.   COUNTIES WITH A WEAK EMPHASIS
ON RUGBY UNION

| County | Index | One club per | No. of clubs |
|---|---|---|---|
| Greater Manchester | 0.25 | 105,772 | 25 |
| Northumberland | 0.28 | 94,439 | 6 |
| Derbyshire | 0.41 | 64,495 | 14 |
| Norfolk | 0.47 | 56,262 | 12 |
| South Yorkshire | 0.47 | 56,262 | 23 |
| Tyne and Wear | 0.56 | 47,220 | 25 |
| Lincolnshire | 0.60 | 44,072 | 12 |
| Merseyside | 0.61 | 43,349 | 36 |
| Staffordshire | 0.61 | 43,349 | 23 |
| Hampshire | 0.62 | 42,650 | 34 |
| Humberside | 0.62 | 42,650 | 20 |
| West Midlands | 0.62 | 42,650 | 65 |
| Berkshire | 0.63 | 41,973 | 16 |
| Dorset | 0.63 | 41,973 | 14 |
| Suffolk | 0.63 | 41,973 | 14 |
| Greater London | 0.67 | 39,467 | 178 |
| Lancashire | 0.68 | 38,887 | 35 |

*Source of original data:* Rugby Union, Welsh Rugby Union, Scottish Rugby Union
(1979).

Secondly, from the 1880s many thousands of immigrants from the rugby strongholds of Gloucestershire, Somerset and Devon poured into the rapidly expanding industrial towns of South Wales. For these two reasons, 'it was from the west country that Welsh rugby received its greatest stimulus'.[13] Indeed, the link between the two regions continued into the inter-war years with unemployed Welsh players being offered jobs with the corporations of Torquay and Weston-super-Mare (in the 1930s Weston R.U.F.C., was nicknamed 'Weston Welsh').[14]

A third reason for the localisation of rugby in the south was that soccer was retarded from developing in South Wales from the mid-1870s because of the apparent unwillingness of South Wales football officials to engage in dialogue with their North Wales counterparts over the composition of Welsh international teams. Smith and Williams note that 'it was nearly thirty years before soccer began to make any headway against the massive dominance of rugby football in South Wales.'[15]

Just as South Wales was influenced by its juxtaposition to the south-west, 'identical preconditions of geography and east-west communications determined that North Wales was drawn increasingly closer to soccer-playing Merseyside'[16] (note Fig. 4.9). The development of rugby in North Wales has been a relatively recent affair, associated perhaps with increased television coverage of the game in the 1960s and possibly the growing need for a national (as opposed to a solely South Welsh) identity in the 1970s. Even so, Clwyd possesses only an average *per capita* index of 1.04.

Only a small number of the Home Counties possess *per capita* indices above the national norm. This is surprising since the region was the traditional focus of amateur rugby, and possesses something of a 'rugger' image. Surrey (1.38) is the major county in the south-east, but as Fig. 6.6 shows, there is no suggestion of a suburban rugby ring around the metropolis. In the West Midlands, only Warwickshire (1.47) goes any way towards suggesting any degree of localisation of the sport in the suburban counties. Indeed, some of the outer metropolitan areas (e.g. Hampshire, Berkshire and Suffolk) have very low indices.

The most dramatic under-emphasis on rugby is found in the north of England and in a semi-circle around the Midlands stretching from Merseyside, through East Anglia to Greater London and thence to Dorset. With the exception of Cumbria, no English county north of a line joining the Mersey and the Wash has an index of more than 1.00. Of the metropolitan counties, only Cleveland has an index of more than 0.70. The absence of rugby from much of the north of

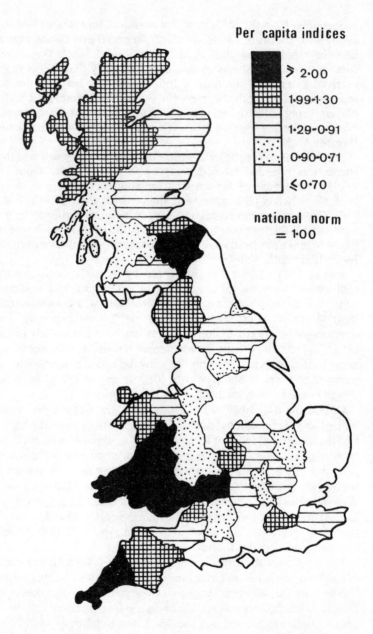

Fig. 6.6. *Per capita* emphasis on rugby union, 1980 (*source of data*: see Table 6.2).

England may be attributed to the intervening interest in the League game in much of this area and in metropolitan areas opportunities for almost all sports fall below the national average.

In Wales nearly 13 per cent of the adult population paid to watch rugby in 1974, compared with the national figures of 2.8 per cent.[17] South Wales is the undeniable centre of rugby union in Britain, Dyfed (the area around Llanelli particularly) and Gwent having about six times more rugby clubs per head of the population than Great Britain as a whole. The only counties outside Wales with more than twice the national average are Borders, Cornwall and Gloucestershire. To a large extent, the objective analysis of the localisation of rugby fits the perceived image: Wales really is dominant, to the extent that the union game has almost the primacy that rugby league has in the north of England. As such, both sports are undeniable parts of regional culture and consciousness.

## REFERENCES

1. Dunning and Sheard (1976).
2. Quoted in Keating (1979).
3. Morgan (1977).
4. This section is inspired by Dunning and Sheard (1976 and 1979).
5. Dunning and Sheard (1976).
6. Dunning and Sheard (1979), 228.
7. The inspiration for this paragraph is Macklin (1974).
8. Barker (1977).
9. Fitzpatrick (1978).
10. Thaman (1973).
11. Smith and Williams (1980).
12. ibid.
13. ibid.
14. ibid.
15. ibid.
16. ibid.
17. I.P.C. (1975).

# 7

## CRICKET: THE SUMMER SPORT

Cricket is often regarded as the quintessential game of England. It has been described, rightly or wrongly, as 'an expression of the national character and, as such, inscrutable.'[1] Cricket seems to have grown out of the English countryside. In the words of Neville Cardus, 'in every English village a cricket field is as much part of the landscape as the old church.'[2] The sound of leather against willow might well be said to herald the arrival of English summertime. Yet it can be argued that a *regional* image has also been communicated about cricket. Some parts of the country possess stronger cricketing associations than others. The cricket match in *England, their England* took place in Kent,[3] and the 'Tillingfold' of Hugh de Selincourt's *The Cricket Match* 'lies in a hollow under the Downs'[4] in Sussex. The scene of R.C. Sherriff's *Badger's Green* also has a downland location.[5] Indeed, Cardus 'heard folk from the south say of cricket at Sheffield that it is simply *not* cricket. Their preference has been for the game played with trees and country graciousness around.'[6] The regional image of cricket is largely southern. Based on the method described in Chapter 3 and already exemplified for rugby in Fig. 6.2, it can be seen from the map of Britain's perceptual cricket region (Fig. 7.1) that the south-east is associated with cricket by over 70 per cent of respondents. However, the gradual decline in cricket imagery as one moves northwards is interrupted in Yorkshire by a 'dome' of activity, associated with cricket by over 60 per cent of respondents. We shall be concerned in this chapter with assessing the accuracy of this mental map and with seeking to trace the geographical growth of the sport, noting its southern origins and establishing the extent to which it may still be associated with the south of England. Consideration is also given to the spatial (or geographical) aspects of county cricket, and, briefly, to the locational pattern of women's cricket.

### *'Village cricket': origins, diffusion and location*

Cricket, like many other sports, originated as a folk game which was widespread but geographically differentiated until the late seventeenth century. The antecedents of modern cricket have been amply described;[7] we are concerned here only with its geographical origins. Brookes suggests that clues to the game's origin can be obtained

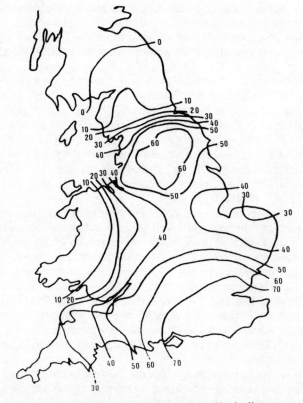

Fig. 7.1. A mental map of British cricket. The isolines represent the degree to which respondents identified different parts of the country with cricket (numerals refer to percentages).

by examining the etymology of some of the game's vocabulary. 'Wicket', for example, is part of Sussex dialect and refers to the entrance to a downland sheep pen; 'beil', which comes from Sussex and Kent, refers to a moveable crossbar into the pen; 'stump', in Sussex and Hampshire dialect, meant part of a fallen tree.[8] Several writers identify the south-east as the home of cricket. Gale hypothesised that the game spread within the counties of that region as a result of the meeting of hop farmers at the annual fairs,[9] but no empirical evidence was provided to support this hypothesis.

Modern sports differ from folk-games in that they possess standardised rules, are administered by a bureaucracy, and have a concern for quantification and records.[10] 'By 1750 . . . cricket . . . was no longer the folk game of old.'[11] The diffusion of a more advanced form of the game resulted from aristocratic involvement, which began in the second half of the eighteenth century. The aristocracy saw in cricket a way of acting out personal rivalries without recourse to duelling, a form of entertainment which could satisfy the desire for gambling, and a means of maintaining contact not only with old friends but also with the workers on their own estates. As early as 1727 Articles of Agreement were drawn up which attempted to impose a standard code of rules upon the game's numerous regional variations, representing one of the earliest forms of bureaucratic involvement in British sport. In 1788 the Marylebone Cricket Club (MCC) produced its first set of rules. By 1800 the folk-game had been almost completely replaced by a more standardised form of cricket which would be easily recognisable as such today. But what of the game's geography?

Many histories of cricket allude to its continued localisation in the South-East of England until well into the nineteenth century. By 1800, Pycroft, in his classic book *The Cricket Field*,[12] recognised that cricket had become 'the common practice of the common people in Hampshire, Surrey, Sussex and Kent and had been introduced into adjoining counties; and though we cannot trace its continuity beyond Rutlandshire and Burley Park, certainly it had been long familiar to men of Leicester and Nottingham, as well as Sheffield.' While it was from the southern counties that the game spread, by 1820 'a small circle around London would still comprise the finest players.'[13]

A rather more precise analysis of the localisation of cricket in pre-Victorian times can be undertaken by examining the entries in G.B. Buckley's gazetteers of cricket references for before 1836.[14] It seems likely that during the late eighteenth and early nineteenth centuries, more than 1,000 cricket clubs existed in England and Wales, the geographical distribution of which provides some insights into the degree of localisation of the sport at that time. Kent (159 clubs), Sussex (109), Hampshire (88), Essex (86) and Surrey (59) were the most prolific counties while Yorkshire, Middlesex and Norfolk also possessed over forty clubs each. Much of north-west England was a cricketing desert: twenty-four clubs were recorded in Cheshire, Lancashire, Westmorland and Cumberland together, and the game does not appear to have reached the two last-named counties until the late 1820s.[15] If variations in population (as at the time of the 1831 census) are taken into account, a *per capita* index of 1.00 may be used to represent the national average provision of clubs at one per 13,600 people. In *per capita* terms, the south-east was an even more prominent focus of cricket activity than the absolute figure suggests. Surrey was the *per capita* leader with an index of 6.69, followed by

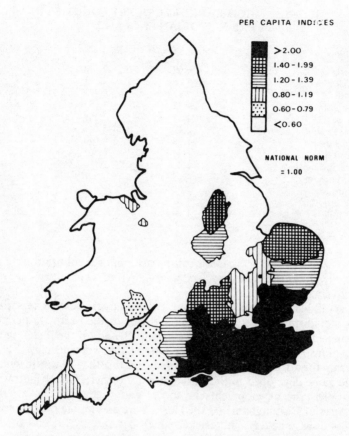

Fig. 7.2. The localisation of cricket in pre-Victorian England (*source*: Bale, 1981*a*).

Sussex (5.48), Kent (5.39), Hampshire (4.32) and Essex (4.31). The remaining centres, with indices of over 1.20 are shown in Table 7.1.

The overall pattern of emphasis is shown in Fig. 7.2. While London clearly underemphasised cricket, the general pattern is one of progressively less emphasis on the game towards the north-west. This pattern is an invitation to modify slightly the concept of a single-feature region described in Chapter 3, and suggests that sports regions may possess an anatomy or structure, akin to what the geographer Meinig termed a culture region. Such regions, he argued,[16] possessed a core, a domain and a sphere — concentric zones of progressively decreasing emphasis on the particular culture in question. Clearly, cricket in pre-Victorian England can be interpreted in this

Table 7.1.    HIGH-RANKING CRICKET COUNTIES IN
PRE-VICTORIAN ENGLAND

| County | Per capita index | One club per | No. of clubs |
|---|---|---|---|
| Surrey | 6.69 | 2,040 | 59 |
| Sussex | 5.48 | 2,373 | 109 |
| Kent | 5.39 | 2,497 | 159 |
| Hampshire | 4.32 | 3,165 | 88 |
| Essex | 4.31 | 3,168 | 86 |
| Berkshire | 2.42 | 5,642 | 26 |
| Oxfordshire | 1.69 | 8,040 | 13 |
| Norfolk | 1.54 | 8,865 | 42 |
| Buckinghamshire | 1.48 | 9,170 | 16 |
| Nottingham | 1.45 | 9,391 | 24 |
| Wiltshire | 1.38 | 9,880 | 24 |
| Leicestershire | 1.32 | 10,367 | 19 |
| Suffolk | 1.20 | 11,397 | 26 |

Source: Bale, 1981a.

way with a cultural core in the south-east, minor acculturations (e.g. Cornwall) at the periphery, and a domain into which the game was actively being diffused.

As England became increasingly urbanised, cricket was regarded as a civilising influence in the new towns of the north, 'a perfect vehicle for the myths of Merrie England,'[17] and for the fostering of religious and educational ethics among the working class. This meant the diffusion of cricket from south to north. The way in which the game developed in the Midland and northern industrial towns parallels the developments in soccer and rugby. In cricket 'the masses of Birmingham and the North were developing the tradition of serious, one-day club cricket which became, by the end of the century, League Cricket.'[18] But no conflict between professional and amateur occurred although, as we will see, locational differences in amateurism and professionalism persisted well into the inter-war years. There had long been professionals in cricket, as in boxing and horse racing; according to Allison, 'cricket presented the image of the professional games player as a necessary and admirable, if rather humble part of the game.'[19] There was something of a division of labour on the field of play; batting was perceived by the Victorians as an art-form for gentlemanly expression, while bowling was skilled manual labour, fit for professionals.

League cricket, at the club level, never developed to any extent in southern England; instead, the fixture list typified the participtory-recreational mode of organisation. Well into Edwardian times, the upper class had country-house cricket weekends, and village cricket was dominant in the rural areas. League cricket flourished best in the northern industrial towns. As Dobbs has put it, 'to the country-house set, the very concept of a league had all the connotations of the northern masses swaying, cheering and booing at football matches.'[20]

It remains now to consider the extent to which the localisation of 'grass roots' cricket has changed since the nineteenth century. This forms the subject of the next section.

## *Present-Day patterns*[21]

According to the National Cricket Association, 10, 103 cricket clubs existed in Great Britain in 1980. This figure is an informed estimate, based on estimates for individual counties, since in most counties the total number of cricket clubs exceeds the number affiliated to the county association. In some counties, nearly all clubs are affiliated members of the county organisation; in others the figure falls to below half. It is somewhat surprising that cricket, one of the most statistical of sports, fails to maintain in its bureaucracy precise details about the level of participation. While the data used in this section are estimated, it is important to stress that the National Cricket Association regard them as reliable. These are used in pre-ference to the number of clubs affiliated to each county association because they give a clearer indication of localisation and emphasis.

In absolute terms there is little doubt that Yorkshire is the leading county with an estimated total of 1,500 clubs, amounting to about 14 per cent of the national total. Lancashire, Kent, Greater London and Warwickshire complete the pre-reorganisation counties with 500 or more clubs (see Table 7.2).

Table 7.2.   ESTIMATED NUMBERS OF CRICKET CLUBS —
THE LEADING COUNTIES

| County | No. | % |
|---|---|---|
| Yorkshire | 1,500 | 14 |
| Lancashire | 700 | 7 |
| Kent | 650 | 6 |
| Greater London | 507 | 5 |
| Warwickshire | 500 | 5 |
| Surrey | 450 | 4 |
| Essex | 450 | 4 |
| Sussex | 400 | 4 |
| Nottinghamshire | 325 | 3 |
| Hampshire | 300 | 3 |

*Source:* Summary of survey of county cricket associations membership, 1980, National Cricket Association. Unpublished data kindly made available by Mr. F.Elliott.

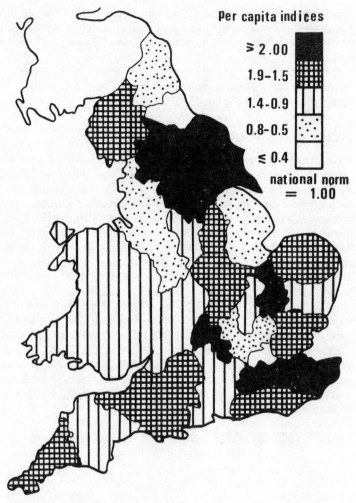

Fig. 7.3. *Per capita* emphasis on club cricket, based on number of
clubs per county (*source of data*: see Table 7.2).

The 10,000 or so clubs which make up the absolute total represent
one club per 5,300 of the population, i.e. a *per capita* index of 1.00.
Applying the index to each of the counties shows that Yorkshire,
with an index of 4.5, emphasises club cricket at about four-and-a-
half times that of the nation as a whole. In *per capita* terms,
Yorkshire stands out as the only area with more than twice the
national average number of clubs per head, north of a line linking

The Wash with the Severn estuary. South of the line, on the other hand, only three counties — Greater London (0.4), Bucks (0.8) and Herts (0.6), — have indices of less than 0.9. Areas within the south of England which emphasise club cricket at more than twice the national norm comprise a broken ring around the metropolis (see Fig. 7.3) made up of Kent, Surrey, Oxford and Cambridge, Sussex and Essex also operate at over one-and-a-half times the national average.

The supremacy of Yorkshire in club cricketing terms forces us to qualify the view that cricket is only part of *southern* popular culture. An experienced observer of club cricket nationwide comments that 'in certain areas, i.e. North Yorks, Cumbria, cricket clubs are very much part of the fabric of community life'[22] and form an integral part of local culture. In relative terms, many of the pre-Victorian foci of cricket have declined in the years since the game started to diffuse to the north. A comparison of Figs. 7.2 and 7.3 reveals that Hampshire, for example, is not as significant in club cricketing terms as it once was.

Interpreted in terms of a sports region's anatomy (see page 71), we may distinguish, in the twentieth-century distribution of cricket, not only the nineteenth-century core in the south-east and the domain into which the game diffused 'contagiously', but also the hierarchical spread of the sport to Yorkshire and the consequent growth of a major outlier of cricket. The area of above-average emphasis in southern England may be regarded as a 'culture hearth' of cricket, with the outlier of Yorkshire actually overtaking the 'core' in terms of *per capita* activity.

An interesting distinction between club cricket in the north of England and that in the south is that the northern game has traditionally been characterised by a more 'professional' attitude to the sport. At the club level the existence of leagues contrasted with the less competitive fixture list of cricket clubs in the south of England. In Yorkshire, the county team traditionally 'farmed out' its professionals with the league clubs, while until quite recently even county cricket in the south was dominated by Oxbridge amateurs (see below). As one northern player who moved south remarked, 'I'd never heard of a "friendly" game before I came south.'[23]

This section has noted the historical shift in the emphasis on cricket at the grass-roots level from south to north. As such, it exemplifies a form of cultural diffusion. What is particularly noteworthy, however, is that the north was far from equally affected. To the north of Yorkshire, Durham and Northumberland operate at about half the national average with indices of 0.6 and 0.4 respectively. To the south Lincolnshire (0.8), Lancashire (0.7) and Cheshire (0.5) also appear quite different in character. Why Yorkshire should so dominate recreational-participatory cricket is difficult to understand. It is possible that Yorkshire cricket is analogous to rugby in South Wales, inasmuch as it transcends class barriers and therefore permeates society more fully. However, only more research will reveal the full story.

## County cricket[24]

The commercial-consumer model of sport is exemplified in cricket as played by the county cricket clubs which, together with clubs representing what have become known as the minor counties, emerged mainly in the second half of the nineteenth century. The spectator form of cricket developed slightly before those forms of soccer and rugby, but chronologically and geographically there are some remarkable similarities. The first known organisations representing the cricketing strengths of individual counties predate the initial formation of the existing county clubs, which occurred mainly in the period between 1860 and 1900. Most of the counties making up the present-day county championship league had been formed by 1875. While five of the first seven county clubs to be formed were coterminous within south-east England, little geographical regularity seems to exist in the subsequent pattern of county club formation. The chronological pattern, however, is one which clearly approximates to an S-shaped curve (Fig. 7.4), and this model has already been noted in other contexts in Chapter 4 (i.e. Figs. 4.1 and 4.3).

In 1873 the restriction was introduced that cricketers could play for one county only, and nine 'first-class counties' competed for the first unofficial county championship, although inter-county rivalry had started as early as the 1830s and '40s. The definition of what was, and what was not, a first-class county seems to have been arrived at in a somewhat arbitrary way, and by 1895 the county cricket championship had all but assumed its present shape with only Worcestershire (1899), Northants (1905) and Glamorgan (1921) being added later. The Test and County Cricket Board, without operating relegations or promotions, is clearly a fossil from the nineteenth century. In the early 1920s, Buckinghamshire was invited to join the county championship but declined because of a shortage of playing facilities. Devon made an unsuccessful application for admission in the late 1940s.

## Patterns of professionalism

By the 1930s, county cricket had assumed most of the features which are present in the game today. One basic difference, however, which

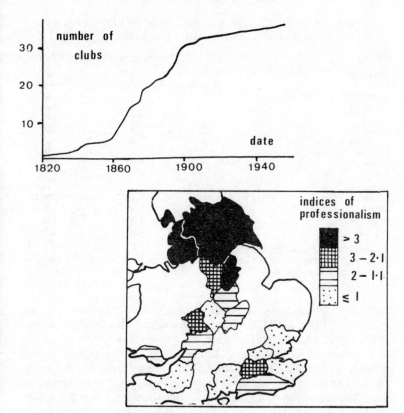

Fig. 7.4 (*left*). Cumulative growth curve for county cricket clubs (*source of data*: Preston, 1980). Fig. 7.5 (*right*). Professionalism in the first-class counties, 1930. The index of professionalism indicates the multiple by which professionals outnumbered amateurs in the county championship teams. Unshaded areas represent minor counties (*source of data*: Caine, 1930).

possessed quite dramatic geographical characteristics, was the distinction between 'gentlemen' (i.e. amateurs) and 'players' (i.e. professionals). The situation for the season of 1930 may be taken as typical of the regional differences which existed in the extent to which the county clubs engaged professional cricketers. These may be established by consulting the lists of county players in *Wisden*, which before the Second World War identified amateurs by the euphemistic prefix 'Mr' while professionals were simply represented by their initials and surnames.

Overall, 219 professionals played with the county championship sides of 1930s, compared with 156 amateurs. Nationally, therefore,

Table 7.3.   COUNTIES RANKING HIGH IN PER CAPITA
PROVISION OF CRICKET CLUBS

| County[1] | Per capita index[2] | No. of clubs |
|---|---|---|
| Yorkshire | 4.5 | 1,500 |
| Kent | 2.5 | 650 |
| Surrey | 2.4 | 450 |
| Cambridge | 2.3 | 130 |
| Oxford | 2.1 | 150 |
| Essex | 1.8 | 450 |
| Nottinghamshire | 1.8 | 325 |
| Leicester/Rutland | 1.8 | 270 |
| Northants | 1.8 | 160 |
| Sussex | 1.7 | 400 |
| Cumbria | 1.7 | 118 |
| Somerset | 1.6 | 200 |
| Dorset | 1.6 | 107 |
| Wiltshire | 1.5 | 140 |
| Norfolk | 1.5 | 175 |

1. Based on pre-reorganisation boundaries.
2. *Per capita* indices are shown to one decimal place because the absolute number of clubs is based on estimates.

*Source of original data:* see Table 7.2.

the degree of professionalism in cricket can be represented as an index of 1.4 (i.e. 219/156). For individual counties, indices of professionalism varied tremendously. In several of the southern counties, amateurs outnumbered professionals in the county sides, whereas in Lancashire (index of 8.5) and Yorkshire (7.0) the county squads consisted overwhelmingly of professionals. Generally speaking, the proportion of amateurs to professionals increased towards the south of England as Fig. 7.5 clearly illustrates.

The amateur sporting ethos of the south-east of England, which is so clearly evident in Fig. 7.6, contrasted markedly with the need of the northern counties to employ professionals in order to compete on equal terms with the more 'leisured classes' of the south. More than 41 per cent of all first class cricketers in 1930 were amateurs, and more than 48 per cent of them played for the six counties of south-east England.

The situation in the post-war years was totally different. Cricket, seemingly one of the last bastions of amateurism, had finally succummed to the onslaught of professionalism in sport. By 1952 only 22.5 per cent of first-class county cricketers were amateur, and for the nation, the index of professionalism had risen from 1.4 in 1930 to 3.4 in 1952. For no county was the index less than 1.7, and for some counties all but one of their players were professionals. Yet the north-south differentiation lingered on: of the seven counties with indices of less than 3.0 in 1952, five were southern, while of the seventy-three amateurs remaining in first-class county sides, 42 per

Table 7.4.   PROFESSIONALISM IN COUNTY CRICKET, 1930 and 1952

| County | Cricketers | | | | Index of professionalism | |
|---|---|---|---|---|---|---|
| | 'players' | | 'gentlemen' | | | |
| | 1930 | 1952 | 1930 | 1952 | 1930 | 1952 |
| Lancashire | 17 | 16 | 2 | 3 | 8.5 | 5.3 |
| Yorkshire | 14 | 19 | 2 | 6 | 7.0 | 3.2 |
| Nottinghamshire | 15 | 16 | 4 | 2 | 3.7 | 8.0 |
| Gloucestershire | 12 | 17 | 5 | 2 | 2.4 | 4.2 |
| Surrey | 14 | 17 | 6 | 2 | 2.3 | 8.5 |
| Derbyshire | 13 | 12 | 6 | 6 | 2.2 | 2.0 |
| Worcestershire | 13 | 13 | 6 | 7 | 2.2 | 1.8 |
| Northampton | 13 | 17 | 7 | 1 | 1.8 | 17.0 |
| Glamorgan | 12 | 17 | 7 | 1 | 1.7 | 17.0 |
| Leicestershire | 13 | 14 | 8 | 1 | 1.8 | 14.0 |
| Sussex | 14 | 13 | 10 | 7 | 1.4 | 1.8 |
| Kent | 13 | 15 | 13 | 7 | 1.0 | 2.1 |
| Middlesex | 15 | 13 | 18 | 5 | 0.8 | 2.6 |
| Warwickshire | 10 | 17 | 15 | 4 | 0.7 | 4.2 |
| Essex | 10 | 10 | 14 | 5 | 0.7 | 2.0 |
| Hampshire | 10 | 14 | 14 | 5 | 0.7 | 3.4 |
| Somerset | 9 | 12 | 18 | 7 | 0.5 | 1.7 |
| England | 219 | 252 | 156 | 73 | 1.4 | 3.4 |

*Source of original data:* Caine (1931); Preston (1953).

cent came from the six south-eastern counties. The changing pattern of professionalism in the county sides between 1930 and 1952 is clearly illustrated in Table 7.4. In both years the influence of amateurs is slightly overstated, since some played only one or two games for their counties.

## Economic geographical aspects

The distinction between 'gentleman' and 'player' was finally abolished in 1963, but a long-standing characteristic of county championship cricket has continued from before the Second World War to the present day — namely, its dire economic condition. As with soccer (p. 31), cricket has for many years been a loss-making economic activity. Even in 1937, the game was losing nearly £30,000 per season, although most of this was being found by wealthy supporters of the clubs.[25] In recent years, Sussex and Kent, two of the most successful clubs in terms of playing strength, have both failed to cover expenditure from the revenue from cricket. Sussex was not viable in 1977 and 1978, even when extraneous income and receipts from test matches and tours were included.[26] The limited revenue received by cricket clubs reflects the meagre takings at three-day county games — an economically anachronistic institution which is also likely to be at odds with the twentieth-century desire for instant gratification in sports.

In his economic analysis of cricket, Sloane recognises that those who run the sport have failed miserably in the marketing of their service to consumers.[27] Improved marketing of cricket has some important geographical implications, and it is to these that we now turn our attention. If profit maximisation (rather than utility maximisation, as in soccer and cricket) were sought, more cut-throat competition might ensue, and some loss in consumer welfare might result, if clubs were reduced in number and some areas were no longer represented in the league (this, as we saw earlier, was the case with soccer). In cricket this possibility was traditionally removed by attempting to equalise playing strengths between counties, despite the existence of considerable variations in population potential. Theoretically, places with the largest populations should be the most successful, and this has tended to happen in soccer with the emergence of the super-clubs (page 30). In cricket, the labour market was formerly controlled by rules on place of birth and residence. The governing body of English county cricket today permits the registration of a player born outside the county if he has met certain limited registration qualifications, and it allows for a number of foreign players to be imported to raise the quality of performance. Restrictions on player mobility might, *theoretically*, serve to equalise competition, but the presence of high income potential must nevertheless increase the *chances* of certain counties obtaining the *best* foreign talent. It is arguable whether, in fact, this has occurred.

Like football, cricket has long exemplified certain sub-optimal economic strategies which possess quite significant spatial ramifications. A traditional feature of county cricket has been what is best termed the 'periodic marketing' of the game over the whole area of the county, rather than the concentration of games at one central ground. Hence, county cricket resembles the system of retailing adopted in the Middle Ages when society was much more geographically restricted than it is today: goods were taken to the people rather than the people coming to the goods, and the periodic fair was a feature of much rural life. Today periodic marketing only tends to occur where there is not a high or continuous level of demand. From the viewpoint of a cricket club, the circular tour around a county in order to play 'home' matches is not only costly, but it is also taking cricket to places of smaller economic potential; and, finally, it reduces the degree of familiarity that players have with their home pitch and thus negatively affects their playing capability.

The typical, but not universal, pattern of county cricket activity in the inter-war and immediate post-war years was that clubs would play their first-class home games at a number of places throughout

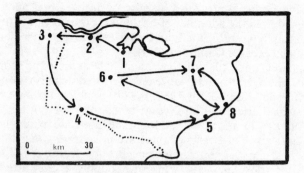

Fig. 7.6. Major matches in Kent, 1952. This map typifies the 'periodic marketing' of cricket, long a characteristic of the game. In recent years Kent's matches have become increasingly concentrated in Canterbury (7); 1 = Gillingham, 2 = Gravesend, 3 = Blackheath, 4 = Tunbridge Wells, 5 = Folkstone, 6 = Maidstone, 7 = Canterbury, 8 = Dover (*source of data*: Preston, 1953).

the season. Often, two consecutive matches would be played at one location, before moving on to another. Fig. 7.6, showing Kent's pattern of county cricket for the 1952 season, is representative of the pattern adopted by what are sometimes called the 'nomadic' counties. Matches in May were played at Gillingham(1) and Gravesend(2) before a 'circular tour' of the county in which two consecutive matches were played at Blackheath(3), Tunbridge Wells (in June — 4), Folkestone(5) and Maidstone (July — 6), with the climax of the season at Canterbury(7) and Dover(8) in August. In other seasons, other locations (e.g. Beckenham and Dartford) might be included, and the 'tour' was not always as geometrically anti-clockwise as in Fig. 7.6. For the seventeen county clubs, a total of 104 different locations were used for major matches in 1950, an average of six per club. Extreme values were recorded by Kent and Essex who played at eight locations each that year, and Nottingham and Middlesex who played all their games at one ground each.

In the mid-1950s, it was suggested in a report on the cricket industry that given the unfavourable financial situation facing many clubs, it would be sensible, at least in the case of the smaller counties, to concentrate cricket at one county ground only, situated in the centre of largest population potential.[28] We may utilise data, collected and kindly made available to the author by Rex Walford of the University of Cambridge, to examine the extent to which the counties have responded to this suggestion in the light not only of increasing financial problems but also of an increased number of matches, due to the adoption of one-day sponsored games (i.e. the Gillette Cup from 1963, the John Player League from 1969, and the Benson and Hedges Cup from 1972).

In apparent contradiction to what might be expected an economic grounds, the overall number of venues increased steadily throughout the 1960s and '70s until, by 1980, 149 different locations were used for first-class cricket — an average of 8.8 per club. In the 1970s, thirty-one *new* locations were added to the first-class fixture list, and it is significant that twelve of these are in counties *other* than the actual 'first-class' counties. This suggests a widening of the spatial margins of cricketing activity in some counties as they attempt to 'colonise' minor counties. However, it is again important to stress that there is no uniform pattern of geographic expansion; indeed many counties have contracted their spatial margins in accordance with the recommendations of the P.E.P. report already alluded to. In other cases, the locational policy of the county has not changed from that traditionally practiced.

We may briefly exemplify these trends. Surrey have introduced six new venues within the county since 1970; Northants have extended their spatial margin of activity into adjoining minor counties (see below, page 86); Glamorgan hold the record for long-distance 'colonisation' by taking games to Aberystwyth, Llandudno and Colwyn Bay since the mid-1960s. These three counties are examples of a group which has widened its sphere of influence since 1945. Other, formerly 'nomadic' counties such as Essex (see below, page 83), Leicester, Kent and, in the late 1970s, Derbyshire (see below) have contracted their spatial margins and are increasingly concentrating their cricketing activity at one location, with others used only once or twice per season and then often only for one-day matches. Yet again, other counties such as Nottinghamshire and, most dramatically, Middlesex, have played almost all their games at one county ground (Lord's) since 1945 and probably since long before that date.

We may consider in rather more detail the cases of three counties which have adopted somewhat different policies on locating cricket in the post-war period. Essex and Northamptonshire illustrate respectively, contraction and expansion of spatial margins of activity while Derbyshire exemplifies also the concentration of cricket at one place in the very recent past.

## The case of Essex

Essex county cricket club may be taken as an example of a county which has spatially restricted the number of locations at which first-

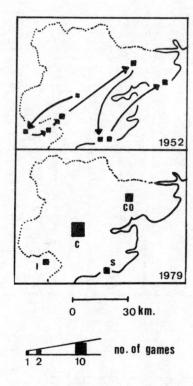

Fig. 7.7. Essex cricket, 1952 and 1979. The decline of periodic marketing and the concentration of cricket at Chelmsford. I = Ilford, S = Southend, Co = Colchester, C = Chelmsford (*source of data*: Preston, 1953 and 1980).

class games are played, even allowing for the increased number of fixtures associated with the more recent trend towards one-day sponsored matches. Lewis summarises as follows the traditional location pattern of Essex cricket: 'Their cricket was played mostly at Leyton, which was rural in the early part of the century. But when London's eastern suburbs spread, engulfing the County Ground, the Essex circus hit the road and the cricket was shared between nine grounds.'[29]

The problem with the periodic marketing of cricket is that much of the paraphernalia associated with the game (scoreboards, heavy roller, boundary boards and so on) has to transported from place to place for games to take place. Essex tended to play two matches (i.e. over a two-week period) at each location, a situation which led commentators to argue that variability in the playing performance of the team was partly, at least, attributable to the absence of a home pitch. Anxious to purchase a home ground of its own, the Essex club finally succeeded in doing so in 1965 when it bought the Chelmsford ground. The periodic marketing tradition has not, however, been entirely broken, and although the majority (thirteen) of the 1979 games were played at Chelmsford, matches were also staged at Ilford (two), Southend (three) and Colchester (four). Lewis suggests that 'there is no doubt that a settled home pitch brought stability,'[30] — an observation which accords with what Edwards has termed 'the home field advantage'.[31]

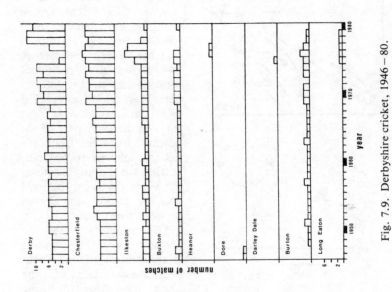

Fig. 7.9. Derbyshire cricket, 1946 – 80.

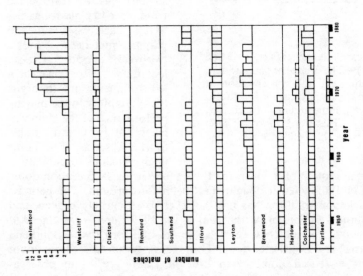

Fig. 7.8. Essex cricket, 1946 – 80.

The Essex situation is summarised in Fig. 7.7. The situation for the season of 1952 is shown with arrows indicating the seasonal pattern of periodic marketing. The tour started in May with games at Chelmsford; subsequent games were played at Brentwood, followed by a move in late June to Colchester, thence to Westcliff-on-Sea in early July, followed by a couple of games in neighbouring Southend and an August move to complete the season at Clacton. Concentrating on the coastal resort towns at the height of the summer may have been sound economic sense. The more detailed pattern of the rise of Chelmsford and the decline of cricket at other Essex towns is shown in the graphs in Fig. 7.8. The case of Essex, then, illustrates growing economic rationality. It could be argued, however, that this has been at the expense of the welfare of cricket consumers, particularly in the East End of London.

## The case of Derbyshire

Since the Second World War, Derbyshire has played at nine different locations, several of which have been tried and subsequently dropped. Traditionally, the majority of first-class matches have been fairly evenly shared between Chesterfield and Derby (Fig. 7.9), with Ilkeston, Buxton and Burton-on-Trent (actually just inside the Staffordshire border) accommodating one or two games per season as well. In 1980 a major development took place which, at the time of writing, remains to be finally resolved, but which further illustrates the economic pressures on cricket clubs to concentrate their activities at one centre. The Derbyshire club now intends to develop the county ground at Derby as permanent headquarters, with only very occasional games at Chesterfield for which the cost would have to be borne by the local authority. A newspaper report in December 1980 vividly epitomised not only the case for stabilising county cricket at one location but also the strength of the sport-place tie which makes sport such a geographically attractive subject. It concerned the defeat of a resolution calling for the retention of 19 days' county cricket at Chesterfield at a 'packed and often highly emotional' meeting of Derbyshire County Cricket Club. The resolution had been proposed by members of the club from the Chesterfield area. The proposer was secretary of Chesterfield Cricket Lovers Society, who said that the society had been told that Derbyshire's plans to develop their ground at Derby as their headquarters would not affect cricket at Chesterfield; the decision to stop playing there had come as a great shock.

He said there had been criticism of the pitch and conditions at Chesterfield, but added that if all cricket were concentrated at Derby there would be a big drop in membership. He accused the club of being 'more interested in sponsors than members', and another member of the society said the club had 'a moral right to allow Chesterfield its share of fixtures'. To quote the report direct:

Derbyshire's chairman, Ron Palfreyman, told the meeting that the resolution had ignored the financial implications of keeping cricket going on a nomadic basis within the county.

'This meeting is about the viability of us as a cricket club, nothing more and nothing less. We cannot ignore cash. It costs us some £5,000 a day to play and we cannot raise that kind of money if we do not have the facilities which will persuade sponsors to back us.'

Mr Palfreyman added: 'The club is now poised to commence its development at Derby and is merely awaiting the result of this meeting before the go-ahead is given.'

Geoff Miller, the Derbyshire captain, speaking against the resolution said: 'It makes sense for us to play as much of our cricket as possible on the same pitch. It has been very difficult trying to compete with other counties who have this facility, and that is one reason why we have been poor relations for such a long time.'[32]

(In early 1981 it was announced that Derbyshire would delay the termination of cricket at Chesterfield and it was decided that for one season only, eleven days of cricket would be played in the town.)

## The case of Northampton

Northampton illustrates a policy quite different from that of Essex and Derbyshire. Traditionally, Northampton has used a number of locations within the county. During the 1960s and 1970s, however, games at Kettering, Peterborough (now in Cambridgeshire) and Rushden were discontinued (Fig. 7.10). However, with the growth of one-day cricket, the county club has embarked on an energetic search for new support in an area to the south, traditionally 'unserved' by a first-class club. Two locations are worth emphasising. Luton, Bedfordshire, is a major urban centre with the potential to support at least one county match per season, and Milton Keynes, Buckinghamshire, has a future population potential of over 250,000 — a size sufficient to support a number of first-class games per season. It is interesting that it has been Northampton and not Middlesex which has been the 'colonising' power in Hertfordshire and South Bedfordshire (Fig. 7.11).

Essentially, Northampton has exchanged locations within the county for ones outside it. With the growth in the number of games played per season, the *proportion* of games played in Northampton has not changed (Fig. 7.11). Whether the extension of Northampton's spatial margins of activity will lead to any wrangling with

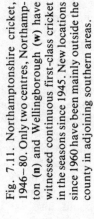

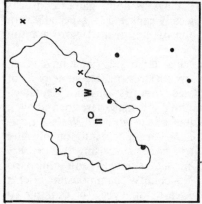

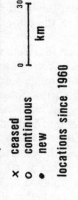

Fig. 7.11. Northamptonshire cricket, 1946–80. Only two centres, Northampton (**n**) and Wellingborough (**w**) have witnessed continuous first-class cricket in the seasons since 1945. New locations since 1960 have been mainly outside the county in adjoining southern areas.

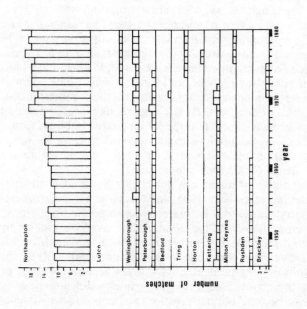

Fig. 7.10. Northamptonshire cricket, 1946–80.

neighbouring first-class counties remains to be seen. As British cricket enters the 1980s, however, this small county's geographical extension of the area in which it plays its home games contrasts markedly with what might he logically expected — especially with the rapid growth in the population of the town of Northampton itself.

These case-studies illustrate some of the trends which have taken place in post-war cricket. Yet it is worth stressing that some parts of the country remain strangely isolated from first-class cricket. Given the expansion of Northamptonshire's interests (described above), Glamorgan's effective 'colonisation' of the whole of Wales, incursions by Gloucester into Wiltshire, by Nottingham into Lincolnshire and by Somerset into Devon, it is rather surprising that neither Lancashire nor Yorkshire has taken matches into the adjoining parts of the country further north. No county championship cricket matches have been played at Newcastle-on-Tyne, for example. It could also be argued that the Potteries conurbation remains strangely devoid of the chance of seeing first-class games — provided, perhaps, by Derbyshire or Warwickshire. Norfolk and Suffolk, with strong cricketing traditions (see Figs. 7.2 and 7.3) at the grass-roots level, have not attracted the interests of Essex whose spatial margins have contracted in recent years.

The seventeen counties, as noted earlier, reflect an artificially fossilised distribution pattern which arguably could be rationalised on the basis of population potential and new administrative regions. In recent years, two quite contrasting developments seem to have been taking place. Some counties have widened and others have contracted their spatial margins of cricketing activity. Some counties have concentrated in single locations because of the economic investment in grounds or because there is a large enough local population to make it possible for them to hope for long-term viability. Counties which lack large populations around their main centre, however, periodically market their service at different centres within the county in order to obtain their support.

In all, the number of places at which cricket is played at the first-class level has increased since 1945, and this in turn has almost certainly produced an *overall* increase in consumer welfare. In an economic sense, however, the county clubs could undoubtedly improve their marketing and hence increase revenue. What form this more aggressive marketing might take is uncertain. Given the 'Packer revolution',[33] gimmicks in cricket may become the accepted standards of tomorrow. Floodlit evening games at downtown soccer stadiums may become normal practice, and even indoor matches might increase dramatically. Both these possibilities have geographical implications which would prove interesting and instructive to analyse.

## Cricket and the weather

The weather has an influence on many sports. In some cases, competition cannot take place except in certain well-specified climatic conditions. Weather and climate act as a physical barrier to the more widespread adoption of certain sports, and sports such as skiing may be described as weather-specific by nature. However, such sports as cricket are strongly influenced by the weather; the game is not postponed and time is not made up if inclement weather halts play. Because regional differences exist in the likelihood of particular kinds of weather in Britain, some county cricket clubs are more likely to be adversely affected by particular weather conditions than others.

The most detailed work on the relationship of cricket to the weather has been undertaken by Thornes,[34] who analysed all the matches of the 1974 county championship and classified them as rain-affected if the wicket was described as 'green', 'sticky', 'wet' or 'drying', or if time was lost on account of rain or bad light. Some counties have a greater chance of rain interference than others, depending on their location and on the order of fixtures throughout the season. The examples of Northamptonshire and Worcestershire illustrate the problem. In an average July, Worcestershire has fewer rain days than Northamptonshire, whereas in September the reverse is true, and it therefore appears sensible for the two counties to play each other in Worcestershire in July and in Northamptonshire in September. On the whole, the western counties are wetter than those in the east, and so are more liable to have their games affected by rain. Thornes suggests that a way out of this problem would be to award compensation points to counties affected by weather interference.

## Women's cricket

The Women's Cricket Association was formed in 1926, which suggests that cricket was a much more socially acceptable sport for women than soccer, which, as we have seen, has been a much more recent phenomenon. Despite its relatively early adoption, however, women's cricket does not seem to have developed significantly. In 1979, only fifty women's cricket clubs existed in England and Wales — the same as at the start of that decade — but the number of schools affiliated to the W.C.A. does show some sign of growth. It increased from forty-three at the start of the 1970s to fifty-one in

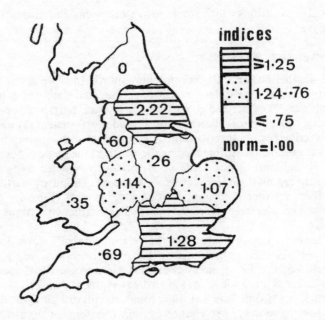

Fig. 7.12 and Table 7.5.    WOMEN'S CRICKET: PER CAPITA AND
ABSOLUTE PROVISION

| Region | Per capita index | Absolute no. |
| --- | --- | --- |
| Yorks/Humberside | 2.22 | 11 |
| South-east | 1.28 | 22 |
| West Midlands | 1.14 | 6 |
| East Anglia | 1.07 | 2 |
| South-west | 0.69 | 3 |
| North-west | 0.60 | 4 |
| Wales | 0.35 | 1 |
| East Midlands | 0.26 | 1 |
| North | – | 0 |

*Source of data:* Women's Cricket Association, 1979.

1979. Only two of the Standard Regions possess more than ten
women's clubs, the south-east with twenty-two being the absolute
leader and Yorkshire-Humberside having half that number.
Together these two regions account for 60 per cent of all clubs
(compared with 48 per cent of all men's clubs).

The *per capita* analysis of women's cricket is summarised in Table
7.5 and Fig. 7.12. Whereas the national *per capita* provision of clubs
is one per 982,000, that in Yorkshire-Humberside is one per 442,000
(i.e. an index of 2.22). The only other region possessing a *per capita*

index of over 1.25 is the south-east (with 1.28). Within the south-east some quite spectacular areas of localisation exist. Buckinghamshire, with three clubs, has an index of 5.71, Surrey (four clubs) 3.95 and Hertfordshire (three clubs) 3.13.

At a general level, therefore, the geography of women's cricket is similar to that of the men's game. Yorkshire dominates *per capita* provision of clubs, and the south-east is the other region within which high county indices are found. In both men's and women's cricket, the West Midlands and East Anglia are also areas of average emphasis, and similarity exists in the lack of emphasis on cricket in the north-east and Lancashire.


This chapter has taken a cultural- and economic-geographical view of cricket. Initially a south-eastern sport with its roots in Kent, Sussex and Surrey, the game spread to the industrial north and took firm roots, especially in Yorkshire. This applies both to men's and women's cricket where, at the grassroots level, Yorkshire is the *per capita* county leader. As such, the present geography of cricket represents an interesting example of cultural diffusion. Yorkshire also appears to 'consume' cricket more than any of the other Standard Regions: a market survey there in 1974 revealed that 7 per cent of the adult population paid to watch cricket compared with a national figure of 5.4 per cent and a figure of around 5 per cent for the south east.[35]

As an economic activity, cricket shares some characteristics with soccer (i.e. both are loss-making) but has responded in different ways according to location, either reducing or expanding the number of places at which cricket is marketed, depending on county policy, but with an overall expansion since the war. The possibility of a Packer-type revolution *within* British cricket should not be ruled out. Will counties merge, or could an alternative league emerge to reduce the monopoly power of the present county league? Only time will tell. What seems likely is that cricket and sense-of-place will continue to be intimately related. As Neville Cardus noted, 'Only on dull days and in dull places is cricket dull.'[36]

## REFERENCES

1. P.E.P. (1955).
2. Cardus (1977).
3. Macdonell (1935).
4. De Selincourt (1980).
5. Sherriff (1930).

6. Cardus (1977).
7. A vast number of cricket histories exist, for example, Bowen (1970) and Brookes (1978).
8. Brookes (1978).
9. Gale (1971).
10. Guttmann (1978).
11. Brookes (1978).
12. Pycroft (1851).
13. Pycroft (1851).
14. Buckley (1935) and (1937).
15. Bowen (1970).
16. Meinig (1967).
17. Bailey (1978).
18. Allison (1980).
19. ibid.
20. Dobbs (1973).
21. This section could not have been written without the help of Mr. F.Elliott whose comments have been most helpful.
22. F.Elliott, personal communication, 1980.
23. White (1977).
24. Much of the data used in the preparation of this section was collected and tabulated by Rex Walford. I am very grateful to him for allowing me to use his data.
25. P.E.P. (1955).
26. Sloane (1980).
27. This review by Sloane (1980) includes many economic insights into cricket and other professional sports.
28. P.E.P. (1955).
29. Lewis (1980).
30. ibid.
31. Edwards (1979).
32. 'Members' Proposed Ousted', report by Mike Carey, *The Daily Telegraph* (London), 16 Dec. 1980.
33. See Sloane (1980).
34. Thornes (1976).
35. I.P.C. (1975).
36. Cardus (1977).

# Part III
# SOME OTHER BRITISH SPORTS

*'Culture, tradition, race, and environment have all worked together to produce a myriad of sport subcultures around the world, and much of this rich material is still terra incognita to the social scientist.'* (Kando, 1980, 293).

# 8

## THE RACKET SPORTS: SOUTHERN AND SUBURBAN

Following the national sports in popularity is a group of activities which are extremely popular either as recreational sports or as professional spectator sports. Tennis, at its highest level, dominates our television screens during the fortnight of Wimbledon; badminton, and more especially squash, are growing rapidly in importance; table tennis is probably Britain's third major sport in terms of active participation. These sports have strong regional connotations. Tennis is perceived not only as a south-eastern sport but also as a suburban activity.[1] One of the aims of this chapter is to review the extent to which the racket sports *share* common locational characteristics. At the same time, we compare our geographical images of these sports with the reality, and establish the degree to which regional provision for participation deviates from the national average.

Each of these sports developed from folk games with origins that are vague and unrecorded. However, one pre-industrial game which continues to be played, albeit by a small number of wealthy participants, is real (or royal) tennis and it is with the present geographical pattern of this sport that we begin our survey.

## Real tennis

Real tennis is played indoors on a stone floor surrounded by high walls and uses a drooping net, and a heavier racket and harder ball than that used in lawn tennis. The sport dates back to the sixteenth century, and the financial constraints on court construction have always restricted the game to the most aristocratic and privileged groups in the country.[2] The location of courts on which real tennis can be played is therefore almost exclusively southern. Apart from courts at Queen's Club (West Kensington, London) and at the Marylebone Cricket Club (North-Central London), facilities are almost entirely restricted to the ancient universities of Oxford and Cambridge and to 'great houses' such as Hatfield House, Hertfordshire, and Petworth House, Sussex. There is also one at Hampton Court Palace, Middlesex. Of the thirteen real tennis courts in England, seven are in the south-east region. The adaptation of this exclusive sport to the growing middle classes of the nineteenth century led to the Victorian invention of lawn tennis, the subject of the next section.

## Tennis

The antecedents of tennis are lost in antiquity. It is best regarded as an innovation which largely democratised the exclusive sport of real tennis. It is possible that the first lawn tennis club was set up at Leamington Spa in 1872, but the game as we know it today dates from the 1880s. The All England Croquet Club had held tennis championships at Wimbledon in 1877, but by 1881 it was growing so quickly that 'the demand for rackets, balls and other implements of the game was so great that the supply could hardly keep pace with it'.[3] Tennis arrived as a modern sport in 1888 when it became institutionalised — and bureaucratised — with the formation of the Lawn Tennis Association.

From the start, tennis was designed with the suburban middle classes in mind. Lincoln Allison writes: 'Lawn tennis as a specific adaptation of the game of kings and courtiers to the possibilities of the suburban lawn was clearly recognised. . . . The Honourable Alfred Lyttelton pointed out that "every country house and most suburban villas" could provide the facilities for lawn tennis, while for real tennis "such a panoply is needed that a royal income must be won to provide it".'[4] The extent to which tennis continues to be a suburban phenomenon forms the subject of much of the rest of this section.

By 1922 there were over 400 tennis clubs and about 10,000 serious participants. By the mid-1930s the 2,874 clubs accommodated about 75,000 members.[5] In terms of the total number of clubs tennis is today the fifth sport in order of importance in Britain. Among women it is the second most popular sport watched on television. It seems likely that the number of serious active participants exceeds 150,000. Professional tennis provides massive prize money,

Wimbledon alone paying out in 1979 more than £260,000,[5] representing a tenfold increase over 1969. This growth in professional tennis is not matched by a spectacular increase in the number of clubs at grassroots level. Throughout the 1960s, the number of clubs fell steadily from 3,197 in 1965 to 2,642 in 1979. Of course, this does not necessarily mean that the number of participants is also declining, but it is likely that many former or potential players have defected to the indoor sports, which are dealt with subsequently in this chapter. However, at the school level tennis seems to be growing. The fact that the number of schools in England and Wales which are affiliated to the Lawn Tennis Association has increased from 1,447 in 1965 to 1,905 in 1979 suggests that the grass roots of the sports are not in an unhealthy state.

In tennis, as with other sports where analysis is undertaken using the number of *clubs* per county, caution is needed in analysing the results of any geographical survey. According to the Lawn Tennis Association rules, a tennis club is 'an organisation of not less than 20 persons, of whom at least ten are of the age of 18 or over, associated together for the purpose (either solely or *inter alia*) of playing lawn tennis'.[6] Clubs will obviously vary greatly in size and in number of *active* members. Hence, numbers of clubs per county constitute a somewhat crude indicator of emphasis but a reliable indicator of opportunity to play. Even this approach ignores the distinction between open and closed clubs; which clubs open their doors to all applicants is not made clear from the available data, which therefore have to be interpreted with care.

There is no doubt that in absolute terms the principal focus of tennis activity is the south of England. The six southern counties among the top ten tennis counties account for 29.4 of the total number of clubs in Britain. The other main concentrations are in the West Midlands and Central Scotland (Table 8.1). The *per capita* index, more appropriate in this case, reveals that south-eastern counties such as Surrey (index of 3.76), Kent (2.48), Bucks (2.07) and Oxford (1.80) have substantially more tennis clubs per head of the population than Britain as a whole (1 per 21,169). Other southern counties, while being generally above average in the provision of tennis clubs, possess lower *per capita* indices than, say, Shropshire (2.53), Suffolk (2.34) and the Scottish Borders (2.04).

Low emphasis on tennis is found in the industrial centres of Britain and the rural periphery of Wales and Scotland. The only exceptions to this are the Welsh and Scottish counties abutting the English borders. The right-hand side of Table 8.2 contrasts sharply with the left-hand side in the character and location of the counties showing, respectively, a weak and a strong emphasis on tennis.

Table 8.1.  TOP TEN TENNIS COUNTIES ACCORDING TO
NUMBER OF CLUBS

|  | Clubs | % |
|---|---|---|
| Greater London | 178 | 6.7 |
| Surrey | 178 | 6.7 |
| Kent | 170 | 6.4 |
| West Midlands | 114 | 4.3 |
| Essex | 92 | 3.7 |
| Gloucester | 85 | 3.2 |
| Strathclyde | 80 | 3.0 |
| Merseyside | 75 | 2.8 |
| Greater Manchester | 71 | 2.7 |
| Hampshire/Isle of Wight | 71 | 2.7 |

*Source of original data:* L.T.A. Handbook (1979).

A contrast between adult recreational tennis and school tennis
may be drawn by comparing Fig. 8.1 with a map of the geography of
school tennis (Fig. 8.2). While in general terms the maps are similar,
with strong emphasis in southern and eastern England, there are
some differences between the maps which suggest that involvement
in tennis at one level is not being followed through at the other. For
example, Dorset has two-and-one-third times as many schools
affiliated to the L.T.A. than might be expected for its population,
while in terms of the provision of clubs for adult tennis, the county is
operating at about the national *per capita* average. Other counties
which exemplify the mis-match between adult and school tennis
include Gloucester and Berkshire. The identification of these, and
other differences between Figs. 8.1 and 8.2 are important, since
through them we may recognise which areas best qualify for scarce
financial help in aiding young tennis-players.

Table 8.2.  THE EXTREMES OF EMPHASIS ON TENNIS
IN BRITAIN

| Top ten counties | | Bottom ten counties | |
|---|---|---|---|
| County | Index | County | Index |
| Surrey | 3.76 | Cleveland | 0.56 |
| Shropshire | 2.53 | Greater Manchester | 0.56 |
| Kent | 2.48 | Greater London | 0.56 |
| Suffolk | 2.34 | Durham | 0.55 |
| Bucks | 2.07 | Tyne and Wear | 0.55 |
| Border | 2.04 | Dyfed | 0.51 |
| Dumfries/Galloway | 1.99 | Gwent | 0.44 |
| Oxford | 1.80 | Highland | 0.44 |
| Gloucester | 1.76 | Humberside | 0.42 |
| Northamptonshire | 1.67 | Mid-Glamorgan | 0.39 |

*Source of original data:* see Table 8.5.

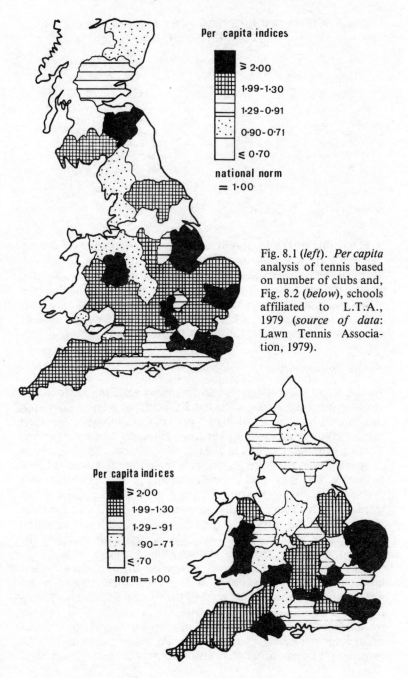

Per capita indices

≥ 2·00

1·99–1·30

1·29–0·91

0·90–0·71

≤ 0·70

national norm
= 1·00

Fig. 8.1 (*left*). *Per capita* analysis of tennis based on number of clubs and, Fig. 8.2 (*below*), schools affiliated to L.T.A., 1979 (*source of data*: Lawn Tennis Association, 1979).

Per capita indices

≥ 2·00

1·99–1·30

1·29– ·91

·90– ·71

≤ ·70

norm = 1·00

Table 8.3.   SCHOOL TENNIS: PER CAPITA ANALYSIS OF
TOP TEN COUNTIES

|  | Index | Number |
|---|---|---|
| Suffolk | 4.54 | 98 |
| Norfolk | 3.15 | 78 |
| Gloucester | 2.72 | 50 |
| Powys | 2.64 | 10 |
| Kent | 2.57 | 139 |
| Dorset | 2.37 | 51 |
| Hertfordshire | 2.09 | 73 |
| Berkshire | 2.03 | 50 |
| Cornwall | 1.97 | 30 |
| Surrey | 1.79 | 67 |

*Source of original data:* Lawn Tennis Association (1979).

The reality of the geography of tennis largely fits the stereotype, Tables 8.1 and 8.2 confirming that it is a dominantly southern sport. Surrey is the principal area of adult tennis activity, and the counties around the capital are all above-average in terms of tennis club provision and school affiliation. East Anglia and Lincolnshire are other areas of high emphasis, while the conurbations (with the unlikely exception of Merseyside) show least emphasis on the sport.

## Tennis in one city

Figs. 8.1 and 8.2 revealed that at the county scale the metropolitan counties generally appear as isolated 'islands' of relative inactivity, surrounded by counties of higher *per capita* emphasis. This short section involves a change of geographical scale, and considers the location of tennis facilities in one city, Nottingham. The location of all tennis courts and other sports facilities in the city was established by Seeley, and it is from his data that the present examination is derived.[7] Here we focus solely on the degree of decentralisation of tennis facilities within the city, and compare it with that for three other sports, namely soccer, rugby and cricket. In this way we will be able to contrast tennis with these other sports with regard to the degree of decentralisation of facilities within the urban area.

For the purpose of the present analysis, the city of Nottingham has been divided into three concentric rings. The inner ring (A) comprises the area within 2 kilometres of the city centre; the middle ring (B) extends 2 – 4 km. from the centre; the outer ring (C) covers the remainder of the city, mainly 2 km. in width but slightly more or less depending on the precise outer limits of the built-up area. In order to compare the decentralisation of tennis courts with soccer, rugby and

cricket pitches, a simple index of decentralisation was calculated
for each group of facilities. The index ranges in value from 0, indicating that all facilities are in A, or highly centralised, to 100, indicating that all facilities are in ring C, and highly decentralised (see
Appendix B).

In the case of each of the four sports, the overall distribution of
facilities was decentralised — soccer and tennis (indices of decentralisation of 67.8 and 66.1 respectively) being rather more so than
rugby (61.9) and cricket (58.4). What is particularly interesting,
however, is the different patterns of decentralisation for different
types of tennis facility. Table 8.4 indicates the decentralisation
indices and the intra-urban distribution of public and private courts
of both hard and grass surfaces.

Table 8.4.   DISTRIBUTION OF TENNIS COURTS
IN NOTTINGHAM

| Type of court | No. | Percentage of all courts | | | Decentralisation index |
| | | Ring A | Ring B | Ring C | |
| Public — hard | 145 | 13.1 | 31.0 | 55.9 | 71.4 |
| Public — grass | 32 | 0.0 | 37.5 | 62.5 | 81.2 |
| Private — hard | 97 | 13.4 | 38.1 | 48.4 | 67.5 |
| Private — grass | 70 | 25.7 | 55.7 | 18.6 | 46.4 |
| All courts | 344 | 14.5 | 38.7 | 46.8 | 66.1 |

*Source of original data:* Seeley (1971).

The decentralisation indices for public courts are much higher
than those for private courts; indeed, a quarter of all private grass
courts are located in the inner 2 km. ring around the city centre. It is
arguable, however, that those people in most need of access to public
courts are located in the very areas where those courts are most thinly
distributed (i.e. in the inner city). Inner urban residents, deprived of
access to public facilities, are therefore diverted away from tennis,
and perhaps from other sports too. Although this is a case-study of
one city only, it is likely that the general pattern analysed in Table 8.4
is typical of most British cities, and goes much of the way towards
maintaining the suburban emphasis on tennis at the intra-urban, as
well as at the inter-urban scale.

## Badminton

Badminton was invented by expatriate British residents in India and,
according to Southey, was 'at first played at Bath, Cheltenham and
other places where retired Indians congregate'.[8] Although the

Badminton Association of England was formed in 1893, badminton remained for several decades something of a minority sport. By 1971 there were 2,909 clubs and 66,500 players. By 1979 the respective figures had risen to 4,753 and 115,277 — growth-rates of around 60 per cent in less than a decade. One club exists for every 10,348 of the population, and one person in 427 is a serious badminton player. As with table tennis and all other sports, this excludes those who play sport for purely recreational purposes without joining a club.

The recent international success of Gillian Gilkes may have stimulated interest in badminton, but growing leisure time and increasing affluence since the Second World War cannot be ignored in explaining the growth of the sport. The average size of badminton clubs is around twenty-four players, and county averages do not vary much around this figure.

In absolute terms, the major centres of badminton-playing are Lancashire (about 10 per cent of both players and clubs), the Home Counties and London, and the Midlands. Devon would appear to be the only surprise of Table 8.5, which indicates the absolute badminton leaders for England.

Table 8.5.   TOP TEN BADMINTON COUNTIES: ABSOLUTE FIGURES FOR PLAYERS AND CLUBS

|  | Players | | Clubs | |
|---|---|---|---|---|
|  | No. | % | No. | % |
| 1. Lancashire | 11,417 | 9.9 | 492 | 10.3 |
| 2. Kent | 8,075 | 7.0 | 336 | 7.1 |
| 3. Surrey | 7,608 | 6.6 | 244 | 5.1 |
| 4. Essex | 6,616 | 5.7 | 295 | 6.2 |
| 5. Hampshire | 5,518 | 4.8 | 214 | 4.5 |
| 6. Yorkshire | 5,185 | 4.5 | 231 | 4.8 |
| 7. Greater London | 4,966 | 4.3 | 229 | 4.8 |
| 8. Warwickshire | 4,693 | 4.1 | 198 | 4.2 |
| 9. Sussex | 3,771 | 3.2 | 140 | 2.9 |
| 10. Devon | 3,534 | 3.1 | 132 | 2.8 |

*Source of data:* unpublished statistics provided by the Badminton Association of England (1979).

The *per capita* analysis of players reveals the geography of emphasis on badminton. The *per capita* figures (Table 8.6) show that, as with table tennis, the outer south-east is a principal focus of activity. The appearance of Cumbria in this list is somewhat surprising, and it is a broken band of counties stretching from Suffolk to Cornwall that makes up England's 'badminton belt'. As with table tennis, the weakest areas are the industrial centres of Greater London, Yorkshire and Staffordshire. As the areal units for which data in Tables 8.5 and 8.6 refer are the old county boundaries, the conurbations other than Greater London are subsumed within them.

Table 8.6.   THE EXTREMES OF INTEREST IN BADMINTON
IN ENGLAND

| Top ten counties | | Bottom ten counties | |
|---|---|---|---|
| County | Index | County | Index |
| Surrey | 3.01 | Norfolk | 0.93 |
| Cumbria | 2.70 | Warwickshire | 0.90 |
| Kent | 2.30 | Dorset | 0.89 |
| Wiltshire | 2.11 | Lancashire | 0.89 |
| Isle of Wight | 2.03 | Derbyshire | 0.86 |
| Huntingdon | 1.96 | Durham | 0.81 |
| Essex | 1.94 | Lincolnshire | 0.80 |
| Berkshire | 1.88 | Staffordshire | 0.43 |
| Cornwall | 1.74 | Yorkshire | 0.41 |
| Suffolk | 1.58 | Greater London | 0.27 |
| Buckinghamshire | 1.58 | | |

*Source of data:* as Table 8.3.

## Table tennis

A late nineteenth- and early twentieth-century parlour game, table tennis did not develop as a serious sport until the 1920s. Today, however, it is Britain's third major sport in terms of active participants and number of clubs. It is easily the major indoor sport, but growth has been steady rather than dramatic in recent years. In 1966 there were 7,534 clubs and about 186,000 players. By 1979 the respective figures were 8,539 and 200,000. This represents one club per 5,140 of the population and one player per 220. In England the average number of players per table tennis club is about twenty-three, and the average number of teams in each club is about 2.5. In total the 8,539 clubs support 21,514 teams. Competition is organised in administrative regions of about 300 regional or local leagues, varying in size from the Birmingham league with 368 teams to the Little-hampton league with three.

Taking teams as the most sensitive indicator of emphasis which is available, the major focus of table tennis in absolute terms is Greater London with 1820 teams — over 8% of the English total. This is followed by Essex (1339) and Kent (1284) each with about 6%. In absolute terms, table tennis tends to be a southern sport, half of the top ten counties (Table 8.7) being in the south. The remaining centres are the population foci of the Midlands, the north-west and Yorkshire.

Representing the one per 2,024 teams nationwide as an index of

Table 8.7.  TOP TEN TABLE TENNIS COUNTIES: ABSOLUTE
FIGURES FOR TEAMS AND CLUBS

|  | Teams | | Clubs | |
|---|---|---|---|---|
|  | No. | % | No. | % |
| 1. Greater London | 1820 | 8.4 | 717 | 8.4 |
| 2. Essex | 1339 | 6.2 | 452 | 5.3 |
| 3. Kent | 1284 | 6.0 | 429 | 5.0 |
| 4. Lancashire | 1242 | 5.8 | 517 | 6.0 |
| 5. West Yorkshire | 1168 | 5.4 | 510 | 6.0 |
| 6. Sussex | 815 | 3.8 | 284 | 3.3 |
| 7. West Midlands | 792 | 3.7 | 310 | 3.6 |
| 8. Hampshire | 772 | 3.6 | 265 | 3.1 |
| 9. Cheshire | 608 | 2.8 | 279 | 3.3 |
| 10. Staffordshire | 546 | 2.5 | 253 | 2.9 |

*Source:* English Table Tennis Association (1979).

1.00, the more meaningful *per capita* index reveals clearly that table
tennis is better described as a suburban, rather than a southern
sport.[9] Greater London, while dominant in absolute terms, possesses
a *per capita* index of only 0.53. The neighbouring counties all have
above-average indices, however. The *per capita* leaders and laggards
are shown clearly in Table 8.8. While the left-hand list in this table
has a distinctly suburban flavour, the right-hand one reads like a
roll-call of the regions of the industrial revolution.

Table 8.8.  THE EXTREMES OF INTEREST IN TABLE TENNIS
IN ENGLAND

| Top ten counties | | Bottom ten counties | |
|---|---|---|---|
| County | Index | County | Index |
| Buckinghamshire | 2.09 | Durham | 0.64 |
| Essex | 1.90 | West Midlands | 0.59 |
| Lancashire | 1.84 | Nottinghamshire | 0.57 |
| Kent | 1.80 | Cleveland | 0.57 |
| Lincolnshire | 1.74 | Greater London | 0.53 |
| Cambridgeshire | 1.59 | Tyne-Wear | 0.47 |
| Shropshire | 1.55 | Cornwall | 0.41 |
| Isle of Wight | 1.48 | Greater Manchester | 0.35 |
| Berkshire | 1.38 | Merseyside | 0.34 |
| Cheshire | 1.35 | South Yorkshire | 0.28 |

*Source:* see Table 8.7.

## Squash

The final sport to be considered in this chapter is squash, which is
thought to be one of the fastest-growing sports in Britain. Invented

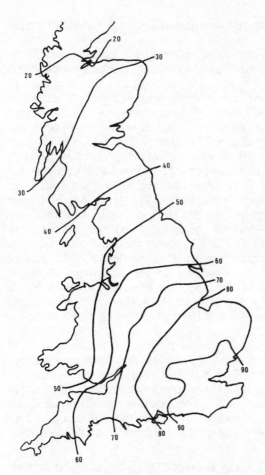

Fig. 8.3. A mental map of British squash. The 'contours' indicate the degree to which respondents identified different parts of the country with squash. From their wide spacing, it is clear that the regional imagery of squash is weaker than that of rugby (Fig. 6.2) and cricket (Fig. 7.1). Squash nevertheless remains associated with the south-east of England.

at Harrow School in 1850, the game was restricted until very recently to other private schools and large country houses. The Army and the clubs of London's West End also possessed courts. Indeed, the first public squash court was opened in Ealing, West London, only as late as 1931. London's West End perhaps possessed the greatest single concentration of courts: in 1938 there were fifty-seven squash courts in twenty-six West End social clubs located in exclusive areas such as Knightsbridge and Piccadilly.[10] By 1947 there were still only 150 clubs in the whole of Britain, and 260 courts. By 1979 the number of squash clubs had increased almost tenfold, to 1,418. It has been suggested that as many as 1,750,000 people play squash;[11] if this is so, the game attracts more players than soccer. It seems likely, however, that this figure overestimates the total number of *serious* players.

While not having such a 'sharp' regional image as some of the sports considered in previous chapters, the mental map of British squash (Fig. 8.3) reveals that it is perceived as a southern sport by over 70 per cent of respondents and as a south-eastern sport by over 90 per cent. The wide spacing of the contours in Fig. 8.3 indicates, however, that the regional identity of squash is not as well defined as that for rugby union (Fig. 6.2) or cricket (Fig. 7.1). The southern image of squash is significant inasmuch as the sport has only recently been adopted on a large scale, and the way in which the image has been communicated is probably through association with other racket sports or through its association with the middle and upper classes. However, the fact that the extreme north of Scotland was perceived as part of Britain's squash region by over 20 per cent of respondents shows that for many people the sport has no specific southern image. The growth of squash in the 1960s and 1970s can be attributed to a number of factors. In an increasingly hectic yet sedentary world, squash takes up little time and little space; it is played indoors; it has a certain snob-appeal; and the international success in recent years of Jonah Barrington may have provided some spin-off.

In absolute terms, Greater London (with 170 squash clubs or 12 per cent of the total), Surrey (sixty-six clubs or 4.6 per cent) and Kent (fifty-seven or 4 per cent) are the major centres of squash-playing in England. The other principal foci are shown in Table 8.9. The *per capita* analysis provides further confirmation that the racket sports are indeed dominantly southern and suburban in location. Two western counties, Somerset (index of 2.59) and Gloucestershire

Table 8.9.   TOP TEN SQUASH COUNTIES: ABSOLUTE NUMBERS OF CLUBS

|  | *No.* | *% of total* |
|---|---|---|
| Greater London | 170 | 12.0 |
| Surrey | 66 | 4.6 |
| Kent | 57 | 4.0 |
| Cheshire | 45 | 3.2 |
| Greater Manchester | 44 | 3.1 |
| Hertfordshire | 43 | 3.0 |
| Sussex | 40 | 2.8 |
| Essex | 38 | 2.7 |
| Lancashire | 38 | 2.7 |
| Norfolk | 37 | 2.6 |

*Source:* Squash Rackets Association (1979).

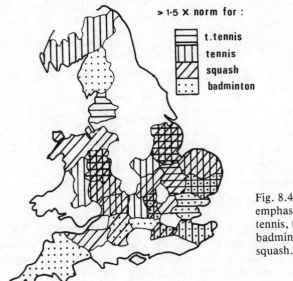

> 1·5 × norm for :

t.tennis
tennis
squash
badminton

Fig. 8.4. Areas of emphasis on table tennis, tennis, badminton and squash.

(2.35), are the *per capita* leaders, these counties having considerably more than twice the national norm of one club per 34,977 people. The other high-ranking counties (see Table 8.10) are, with the exception of Lincolnshire and Shropshire, exclusively southern and suburban in character. Counties having very low *per capita* indices for squash are, as with the other sports considered in this chapter, predominantly northern-industrial. South Yorkshire has only a quarter of the national average number of squash clubs per head, West Yorkshire has an index of 0.42, Mid-Glamorgan 0.45, and Staffordshire, the West Midlands and Strathclyde all 0.50 or less. In addition to these industrial areas, some of the rural counties of Scotland and Wales also possess low scores.

## The racket sports: a synthesis

In concluding this chapter on four popular sports, at least two of which are growing rapidly, we may consider the extent to which they *share* the characteristics of being predominantly southern and suburban in orientation. A final map, Fig. 8.4, attempts to summarise the national situation by indicating the counties which possess *per capita* indices of 1.5 or more for each sport. In other words, the counties which are shaded on the map are prominent in at least one of the sports considered in this chapter.

Table 8.10.   THE EXTREMES OF OPPORTUNITY FOR SQUASH
IN BRITAIN

| Top ten counties | | Bottom ten counties | |
| County | Index | County | Index |
| --- | --- | --- | --- |
| Somerset | 2.59 | South Yorkshire | 0.24 |
| Gloucester | 2.35 | Powys | 0.34 |
| Surrey | 2.30 | Highlands/Islands | 0.41 |
| Lincolnshire | 2.20 | West Yorkshire | 0.42 |
| Oxfordshire | 2.00 | Mid-Glamorgan | 0.45 |
| Buckinghamshire | 1.98 | Grampian | 0.46 |
| Shropshire | 1.95 | West Midlands | 0.48 |
| Norfolk | 1.95 | Staffordshire | 0.49 |
| Cambridge | 1.92 | Strathclyde | 0.50 |
| Hereford/Worcester | 1.71 | Greater Manchester | 0.57 |

*Source of original data:* see Table 8.9.

The map reveals three significant points of interest. First, the sports discussed in this chapter might be most accurately described as being localised within south-central, rather than southern England. A band of counties from Dorset to Sussex fail to achieve *per capita* indices of above 1.5 on any of the four sports. Secondly, the counties of the area north of the Trent are clearly weak in these sports. Of the northern counties of England only Cheshire, Lancashire and Cumbria achieve *per capita* indices of more than 1.5, and in each case this is for one sport only. Finally, the conurbations are, without exception, lowly providers of opportunities for the four sports of table tennis, tennis, badminton and squash. This is graphically illustrated in Fig. 8.4 by the 'islands' of deprivation of Greater London and Merseyside and the extended lobe of the industrial Midlands, surrounded by suburban areas of relatively high opportunity. It could be contended that this pattern is a geographical manifestation of the view that these sports have a middle- or upper-class image.[12] However, the fact that in south-east England a coastal belt which continuously fails to give prominence to the racket sports lies next to counties of similar socio-economic status, forces us to reject such a simplistic interpretation. Instead, such sports might be better identified as part of a life-style which defines a kind of outer-metropolitan popular culture. Perhaps the pattern in Fig. 8.4 represents 'a mirror wherein society can see itself and better understand its character and needs'.[13]

## A change of geographical scale

A basic geographical tenet is that conclusions drawn concerning the distribution of phenomena at one level of scale may be invalid when applied to a quite different level. We have already seen, from the example of tennis facilities in the city of Nottingham, that at the city scale, just as at the national scale, tennis is a suburban phenomenon. But what about the other racket sports reviewed in this chapter? While obviously suburban at the national level, what can we say about their spatial pattern at the intra-urban level? The location pattern of facilities for tennis, table tennis and badminton (but unfortunately not squash) in the city of Bristol has been mapped and analysed by Campbell.[14] Using his data, we can calculate decentralisation indices (page 99) for each of these sports for one city. There is little reason to believe that the results are untypical.

From Campbell's Bristol data we can calculate that tennis possesses a decentralisation index of 24.3. This is a rather low value, indicating a tendency towards centralisation. The cases of badminton and table tennis reflect a quite different pattern, however, with indices of 13.6 and 14.6 respectively, indicating a highly centralised pattern of location. These differences between tennis and the two indoor sports can be attributed to the fact that tennis requires custom-designed facilities of relatively low density. The distribution of Bristol's tennis facilities has, like Nottingham's (p. 99), practically frozen along the edge of the built-up area as it stood in 1920, reflecting the growth in sports provision at this time, and today representing an intermediate location in the suburbs of the inter-war period. Within the urban area, table tennis and badminton are much more centralised as a result of their use of rented facilities and the fact that they do not need purpose-built sites. Being indoor sports, they are free of many of the spatial constraints imposed on tennis. In addition, table tennis clubs are often at places of employment, traditionally in the central areas.

For the case of squash, a *per capita* analysis may be undertaken for the location of 'squash centres' in Greater London, using data from the *Greater London Recreation Study*, undertaken in the mid-1970s.[15] This revealed that, although in absolute terms 62.4 per cent of the eighty-one squash centres were located in the outer boroughs, a *per capita* analysis showed that there was little to choose between inner and outer areas in terms of provision of squash centres. The Greater London *per capita* index (i.e. 1.00 representing one squash centre per 92,000) compared favourably with the indices for the outer boroughs (1.06) and the inner city (0.93). It will be recalled (see page 103) that squash has its historic origins among the private clubs of the West End — the north-west sector of the inner area (including places like Chelsea and Kensington) of Greater London still possessing more than two-and-a-half times the metropolitan norm. The inner areas to the south and north-east of the

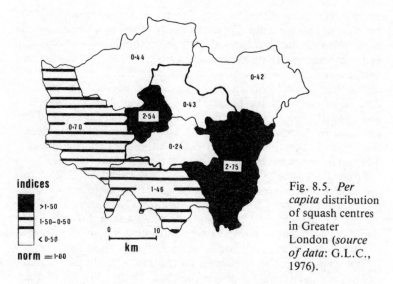

Fig. 8.5. *Per capita* distribution of squash centres in Greater London (*source of data*: G.L.C., 1976).

Thames, however, have less than a quarter and half, respectively, of the *per capita* provision of Greater London. In the outer boroughs too, there is considerable variation in *per capita* provision. While at the city scale the highest *per capita* score (of 2.75) is found in the outer south-east sector, which includes places like Bromley and Croydon, most of the outer boroughs have low *per capita* scores — the north-east and north-west sectors both having less than half of the metropolitan norm (Fig. 8.5).

The lesson to be drawn from the absolute pattern of centralisation of table tennis and badminton facilities in Bristol, and the limited differences between the *per capita* provision of squash facilities in inner and outer London, is that generalisations made about the location of sport at one level of geographic scale may not be applicable at the other. For these three sports, a suburban pattern exists on the national scale; at the intra-urban level, however, this is clearly not so, although the centralisation of table tennis and badminton in Bristol has a different explanation from that of the location of (private) squash centres in central London.

On the whole, the sports considered in this chapter are growing rapidly in popularity. It seems likely that most of the facilities for the indoor racket sports of badminton and squash are currently operating at maximum capacity. Yet the diffusion of these sports down the social hierarchy is likely to be accompanied by a spatial diffusion process from south to north and from suburb to centre. The question of where new facilities are located, in both the local and national contexts, is therefore of crucial importance if equality of opportunity to participate is to be achieved. While still to some extent a mirror of regional culture, it will be interesting to see how long the racket sports can remain the preserve, in a relative sense, of the outer suburbs.

## REFERENCES

1. Thorns (1973).
2. Aberdare (1977).
3. Jackson (1897).
4. Allison (1980).
5. Howkins and Lowerson (1979).
6. Lawn Tennis Association (1979).
7. Seeley (1971).
8. Southey (1897).
9. For a map of *per capita* emphasis on table tennis see Bale (1981b).
10. Horry (1979).
11. Hodson (1980).
12. Irvine (1980).
13. Inge (1978).
14. Campbell (1971).
15. G.L.C. (1976).

# 9

## ASPECTS OF ATHLETICS

In Britain the term 'athletics' is taken to mean what in North America is called 'track and field'. The present chapter considers, besides the well-known running, jumping and throwing events, certain geographical aspects of road running and race walking. Having identified variations in the provision of certain facilities, we also review differences in the 'production' of athletes of national class. The chapter concludes with a view of Britain's place in the world of track and field athletics, and thus considers the geography of sport on a different geographical scale from most of the rest of this book.

### Some antecedents of modern athletics

Open athletics, in which gambling and prize money were essential ingredients, existed in regionally differentiated form well into the nineteenth century. These activities were outgrowths of the rural sports and folk games, to which allusion has already been made (see page 22). Before the beginnings of amateur athletics in the mid-nineteenth century, some localisation existed in the kinds of professional (or open) athletic events in Britain. 'The strongest expression of British rural sports activity' was found in the Scottish Border, Highland and English Lakeland Games.[1] The Scottish games had a strong emphasis on field events while those of Cumbria were more concerned with fell-running. In the Highlands and Cumbria these traditions continue at the present day, albeit in a much reduced form. Weaker versions of these rural sports were found in many villages of southern England and, more especially, the Midlands and north-east Wales. A regional specialism in Lancashire and Yorkshire consisted of jumping events in which the participants were acrobats as much as athletes, while pedestrianism — long-distance foot racing — tended to be focused on the main urban centres of Newcastle, Edinburgh, Manchester and London, the principal centres in the metropolis being at Hackney Wick and Lillee Bridge. Professional athletics, however, never became prominent in southern England, and the 'rich rural professional games culture of Northern England and Scotland was to remain untouched and untapped till well into the twentieth century.'[2] The formation of the

Amateur Athletic Association (A.A.A.) in 1880 had been preceeded
by that of the Amateur Athletic Club in 1866 and by competition
among gentleman amateurs. National championships had been held
as early as 1866. The amateur ethos of the more leisured classes of
the south of England was reflected in the location of most of the
early track and field meetings of any note; and so the annual ranking
lists of the top British athletes for 1866 reveal that not only did the
athletes themselves come overwhelmingly from clubs such as Oxford
and Cambridge Universities, London Athletic Club and the Royal
Military Academy at Woolwich, but also that the events in which
they participated took place chiefly in London.[3]

The A.A.A. did not seem to be a particularly active prosletyser of
amateurism in the north, and until well after the First World War,
amateur athletics remained relatively undeveloped in northern
areas. In 1939, for example, only 401 clubs were to be found in the
north and Midlands compared with over 650 in the south (see Table
9.1). Professional athletics in Britain declined, largely because of the
absence of a central bureaucracy to administer the sport. In addition, no club structure existed, and the gamblers who, in the nineteenth century, had staked large amounts on pedestrians, turned to
dog-racing instead. Rural depopulation and the growing incorporation of the northern working class into the southern sports philosophy also undoubtedly contributed to the fall of open athletics.

It has already been noted in Part II how the amateur spirit was
most strongly associated with the south of England. The southern
bias in amateur athletics continued well into the inter-war years, but
by the early 1960s amateur athletics clubs had become diffused over
the northern and Midland counties. Between the world wars, more
than 60 per cent of the athletics clubs in England were located in the
south; by 1959 the number in the north and Midlands had grown
substantially, although that in the south had barely changed (Table
9.1).

Table 9.1.   ATHLETICS CLUBS IN ENGLAND, 1939 AND 1959

| *Administrative Regions of A.A.A.* | *No. of Clubs* | | *% increase, 1939 – 59* |
| --- | --- | --- | --- |
| | *1939* | *1959* | |
| North | 259 | 435 | 68 |
| Midlands | 142 | 232 | 63 |
| South | 656 | 689 | 5 |
| Total | 1,057 | 1,356 | 28 |

*Source:* J. Bromhead, personal communication.

## The provision of facilities

For events such as long-distance running and race walking the exist-ence of a running track is an irrelevance. Training for such events can take place on a road or a grass surface, but for other events serious training can only be undertaken where, at the very least, a permanent running track with a surface other than grass is available. In the 1980s a track with a synthetic surface is preferable to one of cinder construction. Ideally, indoor training facilities should also be readily available.

The first purpose-built running track was constructed in 1837 at Lord's Cricket Ground in London.[4] By 1850 at least a dozen tracks were in use in the major cities.[5] Over the years the number of such facilities slowly increased until by the mid-1950s there were 137 (public and private) cinder running tracks in England. This repre-sented one track per 300,400 people. The distribution of these facili-ties was very uneven. In absolute terms no fewer than 45.7 per cent were in the three counties of Greater London (thirty-nine tracks, 28.5 per cent), Surrey (fourteen, 10.2 per cent) and Essex (nine, 6.6 per cent). Indeed, the south-east region contained over 56 per cent of all tracks[6]. Greater London, the initial focus of the innovation, was remarkably 'primate' in this respect.

In *per capita* terms, the south-east included some counties with far more than their 'fair share' of tracks. Surrey, for example, had over five times more tracks, per head of the population, than England as a whole; Essex had an index of 3.22 and Buckinghamshire one of 1.57. Even Greater London was unusually well provided with facilities with a *per capita* index of 1.43. In Yorkshire, on the other hand, an index of 0.63 reflected provision at well below the national *per capita* norm. Nottinghamshire had only about one-third of the national average provision, while some of the more rural counties possessed no tracks at all. The overwhelmingly south-eastern concentration of running track provision in the 1950s is shown by Fig. 9.1. Only four counties north of the Severn-Wash axis had *per capita* indices of more than 1.00. Since the mid-1950s the number of tracks has more than doubled. The south-west region, for example, had 2.8 times more tracks in the mid-1970s than it had two decades earlier[7]. The East Midlands had four times more tracks in 1980 than in 1956, although some counties (e.g. Nottinghamshire with one track in 1956 and as many as sixteen in 1980) have been far more beneficent than others.[8] In the 1960s and '70s, however, the cinder track has begun to appear obsolete in face of the development of synthetic, all-weather surfaces, developed initially in the United States. In winter and inclement weather, the cinder surface is all but useless. Synthetic

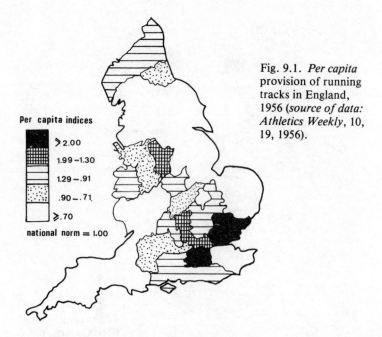

Fig. 9.1. *Per capita* provision of running tracks in England, 1956 (*source of data: Athletics Weekly*, 10, 19, 1956).

**Per capita indices**

> 2.00

1.99 – 1.30

1.29 – .91

.90 – .71

> .70

national norm = 1.00

tracks, however, represent an important innovation, and we will now chart the pattern of their development.

The first synthetic track in Britain was installed at Crystal Palace, London, in 1968. Hence, the first all-weather track possessed the same initial locational characteristic as the innovatory cinder track over a century earlier. As with many other innovations of this kind, the largest city is often the first to adopt them. By the late 1970s, thirty all-weather tracks were to be found in Britain; however, the regional imbalance of former decades remained. In absolute terms 40 per cent were located in south-east England. Nationally, one all-weather track existed for every 1,864,000 people (index of 1.00). In England the south-east had an index of 1.32, Greater London (1.33) having almost the same *per capita* provision as its region. The inter-regional pattern is shown in Fig. 9.2. While it is clear that the south-east dominates England, the *per capita* provision in Scotland is even more impressive, four tracks being located in the Glasgow-Edinburgh belt. Particularly deficient areas are Yorkshire-Humberside (one track for nearly 5 million people), the north-west and Wales, while in East Anglia no synthetic track existed at all in the late 1970s.

Apart from the above-average provision in Scotland, little seems to have changed in more than twenty — perhaps more than fifty —

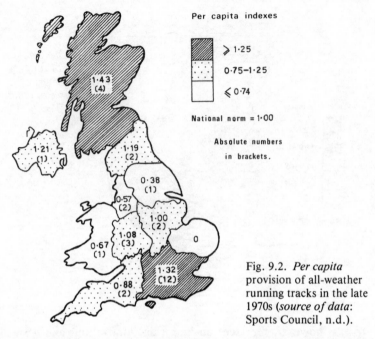

Per capita indexes

 ⩾ 1·25

 0·75–1·25

 ⩽ 0·74

National norm = 1·00

Absolute numbers in brackets.

1·43 (4)

1·21 (1)

1·19 (2)

0·38 (1)

0·57 (2)

1·00 (2)

1·08 (3)

0·67 (1)

0

1·32 (12)

0·88 (2)

Fig. 9.2. *Per capita* provision of all-weather running tracks in the late 1970s (*source of data*: Sports Council, n.d.).

years. The south-east tends to dominate provision for a sport which had its amateur roots there. It now remains to be seen how regional variations also exist in the 'production' of élite athletes, and how particular event-groups seem to characterise certain regions.

## Patterns of performance

The total number of clubs affiliated to the A.A.A. in 1973 was 1,200. However, it is known that as many as two-thirds of these possessed no active members and were, and remain, clubs in name only[9]. For this reason data on athletics clubs are of little use in charting the geographical distribution of athletic talent and alternative data sources have been used in the present chapter. Performances by athletes of a given standard are meticulously collected by an organisation called the National Union of Track Statisticians (N.U.T.S.).[10] The athletes included in such ranking lists are those who might be termed 'national class' and can be said to have a reasonably strong commitment to the sport. For most of the track and field events the top hundred are ranked annually. In 1979 this totalled 1,342 male athletes for whom a club could be identified and may be taken as the total population of top-class athletes. The

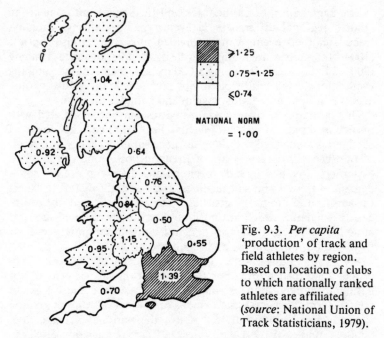

Fig. 9.3. *Per capita* 'production' of track and field athletes by region. Based on location of clubs to which nationally ranked athletes are affiliated (*source*: National Union of Track Statisticians, 1979).

locations of the clubs for whom these atheletes competed forms the basis of the geography of production which follows. Before proceeding with this, it is worth noting that a few athletes reside outside the town in which their club is located, and for this reason standard regions have been adopted as areal units. Even at this level of scale, however, quite marked regional differences in 'production' can be ascertained.

## Track and field events (men)

Overall, the south east is the area of greatest athletic production with 41.9 per cent of all 'national class' athletes belonging to clubs in that region. This is followed by the West Midlands with 10.6 per cent and Scotland with 9.7 per cent. In *per capita* terms the south east is again the principal region with an index of 1.39. Whereas national production is one athlete per 41,600 of the population (index of 1.00), that for the south-east is one per 29,940. Fig. 9.3 shows the geography of track and field athletics in Britain in 1979. Areas of well-below-average production are the south-west, East Anglia and the north. The remaining regions are slightly above or below the national norm.

The aggregation of all the track and field events into one group ignores regional differences in event-type specialisms. Broadly, track and field events can be divided into four groups: sprints (100 – 400 metres including hurdles), middle distance running (800 – 10,000 metres including 3,000 metres steeplechase), jumping events (long, high and triple jumps plus pole vault) and throwing events (shot put and discus, javelin and hammer throws).

On the national scale, certain regions may be associated with particular kinds of athletic events. For example, the north of England is associated with long-distance running, partly as a result of the success in recent years of Brendan Foster and other north-easterners. As has already been noted, different event groups demand different kinds of facilities, and we might therefore expect the sprints and jumps in particular to be associated with the south-east of England, which has not only been the traditional focus of athletics in Britain but also a region with a very high level of facilities, both in absolute and relative terms.

*Per capita* indices were calculated for each of the four event groups described above. For the *sprints* over 40 per cent of the nationally-ranked athletes came from clubs in the south-east. In relative terms also, a *per capita* index of 1.40 reveals that this region is producing sprinters at well above the national average rate. Scotland (index of 1.24) and Wales (1.22) are remarkably similar in their *per capita* scores. Fig. 9.4*a* indicates that the eastern half of England and the south-west are areas of low *per capita* emphasis on sprinting.

A rather different picture emerges from a consideration of Fig. 9.4*b*, which describes the geography of *middle distance running*. No single region is markedly above the national norm, although East Anglia, the East Midlands and Northern Ireland each hover around only half the average national level of production. While the north of England is not markedly a distance running region in *per capita* terms, it is noteworthy that of all the northern athletes included in the 1979 rankings (totalling forty-eight), no fewer than 52 per cent were middle distance runners. No other region had such a proportion of its total number of athletes in any one event-group.

The geography of the *jumping events* (Fig. 9.4*c*) is in several ways similar to that for the sprints. The south-east is the major jumps region, with over 45 per cent of all athletes ranked in the event group coming from that region and a *per capita* index of 1.52. The eastern side of England is again noticeably below average (in a group of events where the provision of specialised facilities is likely to be of importance) in the production of athletes of national standard.

For the *throwing events* (Fig. 9.4*d*) considerable regional concen-

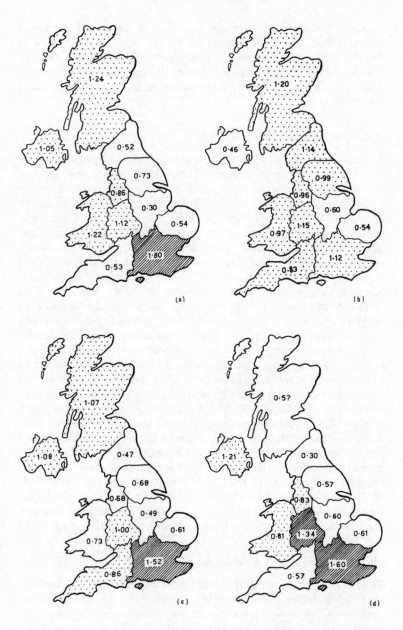

Fig. 9.4. *Per capita* 'production' of athletes in different event-groups. (*a*) sprints, (*b*) middle distance running, (*c*) jumping events, (*d*) throwing events.

tration is found in the south-east and West Midlands. Of all ranked throwers (totalling 299), more than 60 per cent come from clubs found in these two regions, and they possess *per capita* indices of 1.60 and 1.34 respectively. Yet again, the eastern area which this time extends into Scotland, is shown as an area of relatively poor 'production'.

## Road running and race walking

The data compiled by the N.U.T.S. also include performances made over 20 miles and the marathon (26 miles 385 yards). These races are run on the road rather than a track. For walking events over a variety of distances (ranging from 3 to 50 km.) track and road races are included. Although specialist facilities are not required for these events, both long-distance road running and race walking show higher degrees of relative localisation than any of the individual event groups. For long-distance running (Fig. 9.4e), the north-west is the principal focus with an index of 1.61. Although the south-east has more runners in this category in absolute terms (33 per cent of the total ranked) it slips behind the north-west in relative terms. East Anglia appears as a long-distance desert, producing no runners of national level at these events. (This is not to say that athletes from this region who were ranked in the 10,000 metres event were not *capable* of achieving a performance of a sufficient standard to qualify them for inclusion in the 20 miles or marathon ranking lists.)

For *race walking* a highly localised pattern exists at the regional level. Both the south-east and Yorkshire/Humberside approach one-and-three-quarter-times the national norm of *per capita* production. In absolute terms these regions together accounted for 68.8 per cent of all national-class walkers in 1978. The very sharp difference between the *per capita* index for Yorkshire/Humberside and its neighbouring regions of the north-west (0.28) and the north (0) is difficult to explain. It seems likely, however, that a tradition for race-walking has grown up over the years in the Sheffield area and that this forms a part of the overall sports culture of the region.

## Women's track and field athletics

The N.U.T.S. data also permit an examination of women's athletics. One national-class woman athlete exists for every 65,700 of the total population. The south-east is easily the dominant region for women's track and field in Britain, 41 per cent of national-class athletes coming from that region, which also has a *per capita* index of 1.37. It is the only region which produces more than one-and-a-

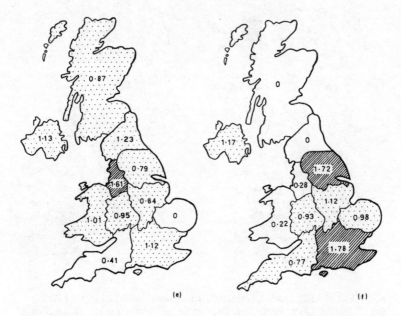

Fig. 9.4. *Per capita* 'production': (*e*) road running, (*f*) race walking,

quarter times the national average *per capita* level of output. The overall picture of women's athletics is that the north and east of England have well-below-average levels of production. East Anglia, for example, provides women athletes at only half the national rate. The north and Yorkshire/Humberside are only marginally better, while Northern Ireland has an index of 0.64. Regional comparison is clarified in Fig. 9.5.

For the different event-groups, the south-east is, in three cases out of four, the major region in both absolute and *per capita* terms. The south-east is certainly as dramatic and emphatic a focus for women's track and field as for men's. Fig. 9.6 reveals the event-group patterns. For sprints and hurdle events, the West Midlands is marginally better than the south-east in *per capita* terms (indices of 1.36 and 1.30 respectively). The south-east accounts for 39 per cent of all women sprinters and the West Midlands for 12 per cent. Fig. 9.6*b* shows the pattern for women's middle-distance running. The south-east is clearly the major *per capita* region (in absolute terms it accounts for almost 44 per cent of women middle-distance runners), followed closely by Scotland (which is also the second major area in absolute terms with over 12 per cent). The east of England is less

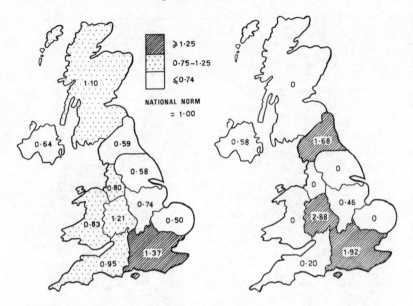

Fig. 9.5 (*left*). *Per capita* 'production' of nationally-ranked women athletes.
Fig. 9.7 (*right*). *Per capita* production of nationally-ranked women race walkers.

homogeneous in this case, Yorkshire/Humberside interrupting a belt of very low *per capita* producers. Significantly, the above-average index for men's middle-distance running in the north is not matched by that for women. Indeed, the index for the north is identical to that of Northern Ireland (0.40).

For women's jumping and throwing events (Figs. 9.6*c* and 9.6*d*) the south-east is yet again the major region. In absolute terms it provides over 40 per cent in both cases, while the *per capita* indices are 1.43 for jumping events and 1.34 for the throws.

Data for the sixty-four top-ranked women race walkers in Britain are also available in the N.U.T.S. ranking lists. Although over 57 per cent of women race walkers of 'national standard' come from the south-east of England, the leading region in *per capita* terms is the West Midlands with a very high index of 2.88 (Fig. 9.7). This index is the highest value of emphasis on any of the athletic events considered in this chapter. A strong tradition of race walking for women appears to have grown up in the Birmingham area, for which there does not seem to be any explanation apart from that of continuing tradition. Men's race walking is not particularly prominent in the region. While only producing just over 9 per cent of women race walkers in an absolute sense, the northern region has a *per capita*

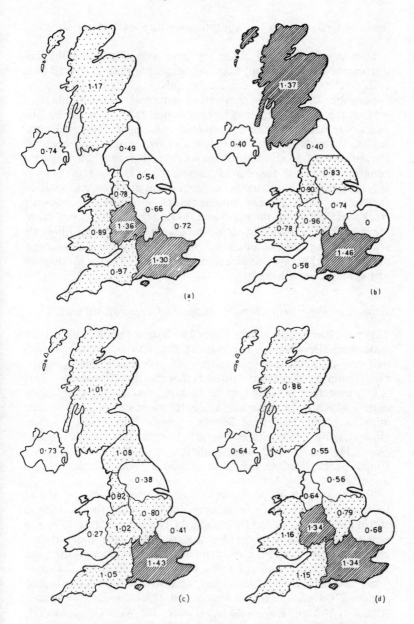

Fig. 9.6. *Per capita* production of women athletes in different event-groups: (*a*) sprints, (*b*) middle-distance running, (*c*) jumping events; (*d*) throwing events.

index of 1.68. An area of localisation within the north appears to be Cumbria.

Considerable regional differences have been identified in the production of élite British athletes. Although the data presented here refer to the situation for one season only, there is every reason to believe that the situation they reflect is typical. Large numbers of athletes remain in the ranking lists for a number of years. The significance of athletic production from south-east England is the principal finding from this section. Of the men's event-groups, this region is the *per capita* leader in four of the six cases. It is in middle-distance running and long-distance road running that it falls to fourth place. It is remarkable that in neither of these event groups are specialised facilities — in the form of running tracks — required. In women's track and field events the south-east is again the major region, ranking either first or second in each event-group. The south of England, for so long the home of amateur athletics in Britain, remains largely dominant in the emphasis placed on the sport and in the production of national-class athletes.

## *Britain in the world arena: a change of geographic scale*

This book has mostly been concerned with inter-regional rather than with international sport. For many sports, however, data on international participation, particularly of world-class participants, exists in almost as great profusion as that for the national level. This is true especially of track and field athletics, where the presence of detailed statistical data permits a brief review of Britain's place in the athletics world. How does Britain compare with, say, the Soviet Union and the United States in terms of world-class athletic productivity? How diversified is our athletic output? What events typify British production? In this short section we seek to answer these questions.

For the present purpose, world class-athletes can be defined as those who achieve a performance capable of ranking them in the top 100 in the world in any of the standard Olympic events. In 1976, the year for which the most detailed analyses have been undertaken,[11] global output of world-class male athletes was about 1 per one million people (i.e. index of 1.00). In 1976, Britain produced sixty-one world-class male athletes, compared with 446 from the United States, 274 from the Soviet Union and 113 from East Germany. Ahead of Britain in absolute terms were also West Germany (99), Poland (92), Finland (67) and France (67). Other countries producing more than ten world-class rankings are shown in Table 9.2, which also shows the more significant *per capita* indices. These

Table 9.2. INDICATORS OF WORLD TRACK AND
FIELD OUTPUT, 1976

| 1<br>Country | 2<br>Absolute<br>output | 3<br>Per capita<br>index | 4<br>1 per 1000 of<br>male population | 5<br>Specialisation<br>index |
|---|---|---|---|---|
| United States | 446 | 4.69 | 222 | 26.16 |
| Soviet Union | 274 | 2.56 | 407 | 27.87 |
| East Germany | 113 | 14.95 | 70 | 24.50 |
| West Germany | 99 | 4.50 | 291 | 25.69 |
| Poland | 92 | 6.04 | 172 | 24.59 |
| Finland | 67 | 31.40 | 33 | 31.07 |
| France | 67 | 3.09 | 337 | 25.27 |
| United Kingdom | 61 | 2.36 | 442 | 28.26 |
| Italy | 38 | 1.51 | 688 | 30.23 |
| Sweden | 31 | 8.00 | 130 | 28.66 |
| Australia | 30 | 4.87 | 214 | 32.86 |
| Canada | 30 | 2.89 | 360 | 26.24 |
| Hungary | 28 | 5.82 | 179 | 35.71 |
| Czechoslovakia | 28 | 4.17 | 250 | 31.94 |
| Romania | 27 | 3.00 | 346 | 35.33 |
| South Africa | 27 | 2.66 | 391 | 34.90 |
| Switzerland | 26 | 8.76 | 119 | 27.72 |
| Belgium | 25 | 5.51 | 189 | 35.55 |
| Kenya | 23 | 4.36 | 239 | 42.38 |
| Bulgaria | 18 | 4.55 | 229 | 36.86 |
| Cuba | 17 | 4.03 | 258 | 36.73 |
| Yugoslavia | 17 | 1.74 | 593 | 29.40 |
| Norway | 15 | 8.10 | 128 | 38.30 |
| Spain | 14 | 0.88 | 1,183 | 33.51 |
| Ethiopia | 13 | 1.04 | 1,000 | 49.25 |
| New Zealand | 12 | 8.73 | 119 | 36.06 |
| Greece | 12 | 2.99 | 357 | 35.36 |
| Trinidad | 10 | 22.25 | 47 | 48.99 |
| Japan | 10 | 0.20 | 5,136 | 40.00 |
| Netherlands | 10 | 1.82 | 571 | 37.42 |

*Source:* Bale (1979c).

reveal that, when ranked according to this measure, Britain's position is much lower. Although producing at two-and-one-third times the global *per capita* rate, countries like Finland (index of 31.40), Trinidad (22.25) and East Germany (14.95) are vastly superior, given their resource base. A number of other countries — e.g. Sweden, Switzerland, New Zealand, Norway, Poland, Belgium and even Greece — are superior to Britain in *per capita* output. However, Britain, with an index of 2.36, is remarkably close to the Soviet Union (2.56), although the popular media frequently denigrate British athletic performance by comparison with Soviet opposition.

The Soviet sports machine is clearly not oiled as well as it might be, to judge by data such as these.

Table 9.2 includes another index as well. The specialisation index (see Appendix C) summarises the extent to which a nation's world-class athletic output is concentrated or diversified among the eighteen track and field events. An equal number of athletes in each event would result in an index of 23.59 — perfect diversification of output. If all world-class athletes were concentrated in one event, the resulting index would be 100 — extreme specialisation. Ideally, nations might strive to achieve low specialisation scores but high *per capita* output indices. Column 5 of Table 9.2 shows that the two Germanies, Poland and France have extremely well diversified world-class athletics squads, since all have specialisation indices of less than 26.0. The British output is less diversified than that of these nations, but is again not so very different from that of the Soviet Union (27.87 for the Soviet Union, 28.26 for Britain). While Finland is prolific in *per capita* terms, her output is rather specialised (specialisation index of 31.07). Patterns in other nations are shown in Table 9.2.

We should finally consider which event-groups individual countries specialise in. It is well known that certain countries are associated with certain events, e.g. Finland for javelin throwing and Kenya for long-distance running. For the continent of Europe, Fig. 9.8 reveals the event-groups which characterised each nation in 1976. Britain is characterised in her world-class output by distance runners, sprinters and throwers — a three event-group nation like the Soviet Union, France and Spain, for example. Sweden, the two Germanies and Poland are among a number of four event-group countries while Finland, Norway and Austria are typified by two event-groups. The technique, known as combination analysis, which was used in the production of Fig. 9.8, is described in Appendix D.

From this brief overview of the geography of international athletics it is clear that Britain, while being an above-average producer of world-class athletes in global terms, falls some way behind several other European nations in terms of both *per capita* production and diversification of output. The British situation is remarkably similar to that of the Soviet Union. Both have *per capita* indices below the European norm of 3.42, both are moderately diversified, and both are typified by three event-groups.

More than a century after being adopted as a modern sport, track and field athletics in Britain remains overwhelmingly southern in orientation. In terms of provision of facilities and opportunities for spectators at major events, the south-east remains privileged in both

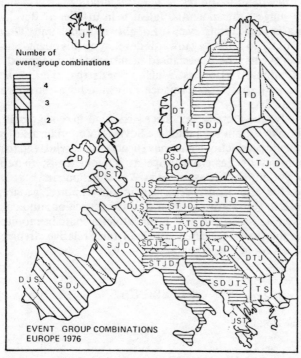

S = Sprints   D = Distance   J = Jumps   T = Throws

Fig. 9.8. Event-group combinations, Europe, 1976 (*source*: Bale, 1979*b*).

absolute and *per capita* terms. In the production of national-class athletes, the south-east also tends to be dominant, especially in track and field events which are strongly dependent on the use of special-ised facilities. It is difficult to resist making a causal link between the provision of facilities and resulting athletic achievement. Where track and field provision is not required, southern dominance begins to wane. Middle-distance running has no region with an index of more than 1.20; long-distance road running is dominated in *per capita* terms by northern, rather than southern, regions; the south, in its emphasis on race walking, is closely rivalled by Yorkshire for men and is surpassed by the West Midlands for women. But as a general rule athletics remains south-eastern in orientation.

Given a random distribution of potential athletic talent and ability, the patterns of regional differentiation described in this chapter suggest that potential talent is insufficiently developed in certain areas for certain events. Equality of opportunity would, on the face of it, go some way towards developing this talent. However, in certain events where specialised facilities are not required, variations in emphasis also exist which suggests that the link between facilities and sports performance may not be as strong as was thought at first.

Globally, the tentative evidence presented here suggests that in several ways Britain resembles the Soviet Union in terms of world-class athletic production. This may surprise those who tend to regard the countries of Eastern Europe as homogeneous; in terms of athletic output they are as varied as Western countries.[12]

Using the approaches described in this chapter, geographical variations in the relative abilities of different regions and countries to produce national- and world-class athletes could be monitored at periodic intervals. A clearer picture of their relative strengths and weaknesses could then be obtained.

## REFERENCES

1. McNab (1972).
2. ibid.
3. Lovesey and Terry (1969).
4. *Sports Quarterly Magazine* (1980).
5. Lovesey (1979).
6. For source of data see Fig. 9.1.
7. South-Western Sports Council (1976).
8. Regional Council for Sport and Recreation (1980).
9. Sports Council (1973).
10. National Union of Track Statisticians (1979).
11. Bale (1979c).
12. Bale (1979b).

# 10

## OTHER BRITISH SPORTS

Hitherto most attention has been directed towards the 'national' sports and those which probably rank as important in terms of participation and interest. The present chapter reviews certain geographical aspects of a number of other sports, the regional patterns of which differ considerably one from the other. Some are highly localised while in others few individual counties possess high per capita indices. Some are peripheral in location; others are more central. But in each case, some counties or regions clearly possess more than their 'fair share' of clubs or facilities and for this reason their geographical patterns are worthy of identification.

Several of the sports identified in this chapter differ in some respects from those already discussed. Golf, for example, takes up much more space than most other sports; motor sports and horse racing involve the incorporation of machinery and animals; and basketball is a classic example of a sports import. The chapter also includes a review of the geography of opportunity for serious swimming.

### Golf

Golf is a game of the east coast of Scotland. Pottinger observed: 'The geology of our island is such that links made of sand which has ceased drifting and has acquired a covering layer of turf are to be found in greater abundance on the Eastern seaboard than elsewhere'.[1] He was referring specifically to the coast of Fife with which not only golf, but innovations in golf, are closely associated. 'The invention of the gutta-percha ball in St. Andrews in 1852 was an enormous step towards greater popularity for golf.'[2] By Edwardian times golf was a growth industry. Dobbs suggests that by 1907 there were 20,000 full time employees in golf (stewards, professionals and so on) and 80,000 part-time caddies[3]. Whereas before 1880 there had been only a dozen or so clubs in England, and the game was played in socially exclusive circles, the total number of clubs had grown by 1914 to about 1,000.[4] Since the 1930s the figure seems to have settled at around 1,200. The adoption curve for Somerset (Fig. 10.1) is probably typical. As with other sports, a slow period of initial growth was followed by a speeding-up in the adoption process followed by a final period of slower growth. The county's total

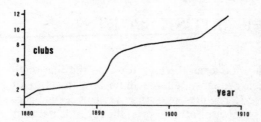

Fig. 10.1. Cumulative growth curve for golf clubs in Somerset (*source of data*: South Western Sports Council, 1968).

number of golf clubs had been established by 1910.

Golf has been described as having a 'voracious hunger for land'.[5] About 40 – 70 hectares (100 – 175 acres) are needed for an eighteen-hole course, which should ideally include gently undulating sites with hazards and traps. The growth of the sport 'represented a major re-use of the landscape'[6], and the presence of a golf course often influenced the siting of the more affluent suburbs in the inter- and post-war years.[7] We may now proceed to the present regional distribution of golf activity.

In Scotland today there are about 400 golf courses and 630 clubs for a population of under 5.5 million while in England the respective figures are just over 1,000 and 1,300 for a population of about 46 million. In terms of club provision, Scotland contains over 30 per cent of all clubs in Britain while two counties, Strathclyde (12.2 per cent) and Lothian (7.6 per cent), together account for almost one-fifth. The counties of central Scotland dominate absolute provision, as Table 10.1 clearly indicates. Other major centres include Yorkshire and the north-west and a group of counties in the south-east.

Table 10.1.   MAJOR GOLF COUNTIES: ABSOLUTE NUMBERS OF GOLF CLUBS

|  | No. | % |
|---|---|---|
| Strathclyde | 248 | 12.2 |
| Lothian | 154 | 7.6 |
| Yorkshire | 143 | 7.0 |
| Lancashire | 133 | 6.5 |
| Kent | 74 | 3.6 |
| Tayside | 72 | 3.5 |
| Cheshire | 69 | 3.4 |
| Surrey | 67 | 3.3 |
| Hampshire | 61 | 3.0 |
| Sussex | 59 | 2.9 |

*Sources:* Scottish Golf Union (1979); English Golf Union (1977).

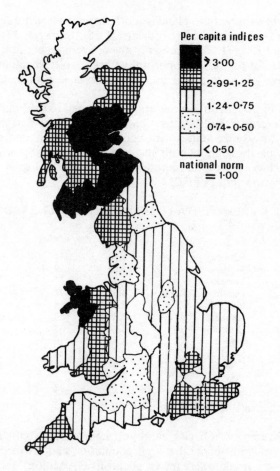

Fig. 10.2. *Per capita* opportunity for playing golf
based on number of clubs (*source of data*: English
Golf Union, 1978; Scottish Golf Union, 1979).

The more sensitive *per capita* analysis reveals that Scottish counties dominate golf in relative as well as absolute terms (Fig. 10.2).
Very high *per capita* indices are recorded for Lothian and Borders,
each of which has an index of more than 5.00, indicating that they
have more than five times the national average *per capita* number of
golf clubs of one per 26,474 of the population. Other Scottish counties, namely Dumfries/Galloway and Tayside, both have over four
times the national norm while the remaining counties in the top ten
include other Scottish and Welsh counties with indices of over 2.5.

Suburban southern England is another area where a broken belt of counties, made up of Hertfordshire (1.35), Surrey (1.77), Sussex (1.26) and Kent (1.40), represents above-average, but not spectacular, areas of *per capita* opportunity to play golf. Remaining areas of relatively high emphasis include Cumbria (2.17) and Cornwall (1.53).

Areas in which golf is weak are concentrated in the English Midlands, Severnside and Greater London. Parts of the East and West Midlands possess counties with under half the national *per capita* norm, while the counties both north and south of the Severn estuary fail to achieve *per capita* scores of more than 0.7. Greater London has a very low index of 0.22.

Table 10.2.   PER CAPITA LEADERS IN GOLF CLUB PROVISION

|  | *Index* | *No. of clubs* |
|---|---|---|
| Lothian | 5.40 | 154 |
| Borders | 5.03 | 19 |
| Tayside | 4.74 | 72 |
| Dumfries/Galloway | 4.05 | 22 |
| Fife | 3.44 | 44 |
| Gwynedd | 3.34 | 20 |
| Central | 3.14 | 32 |
| Clwyd | 2.68 | 16 |
| Strathclyde | 2.64 | 248 |
| Grampian | 2.57 | 44 |
| Powys | 2.55 | 11 |
| Cumbria | 2.17 | 24 |

*Source of original data:* see Table 10.1.

The pattern of golf club (and golf course) location is a classic example of a mis-match between population and provision. Most facilities are found where fewest people live. Additional facilities to meet the latent demands of an increasingly golf-oriented society are most urgently needed in the West and East Midlands and parts of the north of England. Each of these areas requires additions to capacity of well above the national increase which was adjudged in the early 1970s to be about 50 per cent.[8] Being a space-extensive sport, it is important that money spent on the construction of a golf course should be carefully controlled and judiciously allocated, in view of the geographical distribution of facilities described above.

## Men and machines

The technological revolution of the nineteenth century led to the emergence of machine-based sports, the first of the kind being cycling. It developed as a Victorian 'craze', and between the world wars grew rapidly as a mass participatory sport. Newer technologies led to the adoption in the 1920s and '30s of various motor sports — motor-car racing and various kinds of motor-cycle racing. In the case of auto-sports, the incorporation of fuel-powered machinery as an integral part of the sporting activity makes the sport different in its very nature from other sports so far considered. Nevertheless, as Aveni points out, motorised sports share many characteristics of other sports, but are based on the physical prowess of man *and* machine.[9] The concentration and stamina required for motor-cycle and motor-car racing are undeniable, and for this reason we include them as examples of modern sports.

## Cycling

Cycling covers a range of activities from purely recreational pursuits to recreational and professional sports. Most cycling is of a purely recreational nature, calling for limited physical prowess and being uncompetitive. The British Cycling Federation, which aims to 'control the sport *and pastime* of cycling *in all its forms*' (italics added)[10] publishes data on all cycling clubs but because some (many?) will concentrate on non-competitive cycling, caution is needed in analysing the data for opportunities to participate.

In recent years cycling has suffered something of a decline. Before the Second World War, more than 3,000 cycling clubs existed in Britain with over 60,000 members.[11] By 1965, however, membership of the British Cycling Federation had fallen to 11,000, and a decade later to below 9,500. Likewise, whereas there were 3,500 cycling clubs before the Second World War, the present number is 636. The absolute leaders in terms of the distribution of cycling clubs are

Table 10.3.   TOP TEN CYCLING COUNTIES IN ENGLAND
(by absolute numbers of cycling clubs)

|  | *No.* | *%* |
|---|---|---|
| Greater London | 77 | 12.1 |
| West Yorkshire | 44 | 6.9 |
| West Midlands | 35 | 5.5 |
| Essex | 35 | 5.5 |
| Lancashire | 25 | 3.9 |
| Hampshire | 25 | 3.9 |
| South Yorkshire | 24 | 3.8 |
| Merseyside | 20 | 3.1 |
| Nottingham | 17 | 2.7 |
| Cheshire | 17 | 2.7 |

*Source:* British Cycling Federation (1979).

shown in Table 10.3. Three counties, all of them metropolitan in character — Greater London, West Yorkshire and the West Midlands — contain 25 per cent of all clubs.

The more sensitive *per capita* analysis (index of 1.00 representing one club per 77,200 people) reveals, however, that while the conurbations are not as low in terms of provision as with some other sports, opportunities for joining a cycling club are most strongly concentrated in a belt of contiguous counties stretching from Lancashire through the national leader, Lincolnshire (index of 2.04), to Essex. The metropolitan counties provide an assortment of indices, ranging from the very low (Manchester) to the average (West Midlands) to the above-average (West Yorkshire). The northern and western peripheries are noticably deficient in *per capita* provision of clubs, although it would be too crudely deterministic to attribute this to a combination of strong westerly winds and unfavourable relief! The *per capita pattern* is shown in greater detail in Table 10.4 and Fig. 10.3.

Table 10.4.    THE EXTREMES OF OPPORTUNITY
FOR CYCLING, 1979

| Top ten counties | | | Bottom ten counties | | |
|---|---|---|---|---|---|
| | Index | One club per | | Index | One club per |
| Lincolnshire | 2.04 | 37,858 | Northumberland | 0.00 | — |
| Essex | 1.89 | 40,863 | Greater Manchester | 0.29 | 266,317 |
| West Yorkshire | 1.64 | 47,093 | Cumbria | 0.49 | 157,616 |
| Warwickshire | 1.49 | 51,833 | Devon | 0.49 | 157,616 |
| Cheshire | 1.44 | 53,633 | Cornwall | 0.56 | 137,914 |
| South Yorkshire | 1.42 | 54,389 | Oxfordshire | 0.57 | 135,495 |
| Lancashire | 1.41 | 54,774 | Berkshire | 0.58 | 133,159 |
| Cambridgeshire | 1.37 | 56,374 | Durham | 0.63 | 122,590 |
| Cleveland | 1.36 | 56,788 | Isle of Wight | 0.68 | 113,576 |
| Nottinghamshire | 1.35 | 57,209 | Gwynedd | 0.68 | 113,576 |

*Source of original data:* see Table 10.3.

In addition to these regional differences in the opportunity to join a cycling club, the facilities for the rather more specialised activity of track racing are worthy of brief examination. This takes place on specially prepared circuits of between 300 and 500 metres which are often banked for the sake of both speed and safety. The location of specialist facilities is far from uniform. The East Midlands, for example, has more than two-and-a-quarter times the national level of provision, while the West Midlands and Wales are also well provided for on a *per capita* basis. The north-west and the south-west, on the other hand, have only three tracks out of the national total of

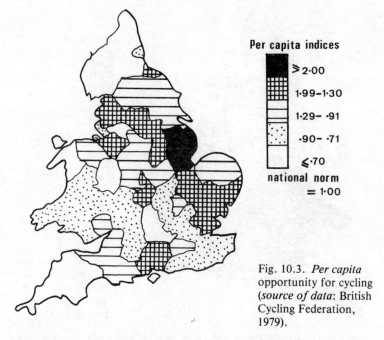

Per capita indices

≥ 2·00

1·99–1·30

1·29– ·91

·90– ·71

≤ ·70

national norm
= 1·00

Fig. 10.3. *Per capita*
opportunity for cycling
(*source of data*: British
Cycling Federation,
1979).

thirty-two, and have *per capita* indices of around 0.5.

A peculiarity is that while the East and West Midlands are very well provided for in terms of cycling tracks, they are not particularly prominent in terms of the *per capita* number of cycling clubs (Fig. 10.3).

*Auto-cycling*

Motor-cycling takes various forms, being accommodated on road, country and track. This section deals with both auto-cycling as a recreational sport and the professional sport of speedway racing. In absolute terms, auto-cycling is a southern sport (see Table 10.5). No fewer than seven of the top ten counties are in south-east England, and seven counties in the south-east account for over 30 per cent of all auto-cycling clubs in England and Wales.

Auto-cycling is, perhaps, the sport in which the *per capita* analysis is most different from the absolute pattern of club provision. Fig. 10.4 and Table 10.6 reveal that far from being south-eastern in relative terms, the sport is dominant in the rural areas immediately east and west of Offa's Dyke. Whereas the national rate of provision is one club per 99,430, the Welsh county of Powys (index of 8.48) has

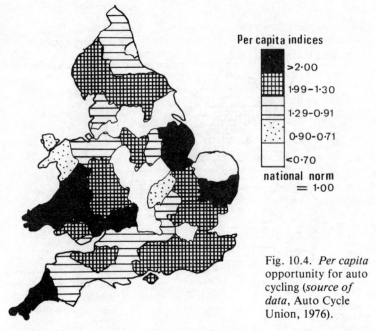

Per capita indices

>2·00

1·99–1·30

1·29–0·91

0·90–0·71

<0·70

national norm
= 1·00

Fig. 10.4. *Per capita* opportunity for auto cycling (*source of data*, Auto Cycle Union, 1976).

Table 10.5.  AUTO-CYCLING: ABSOLUTE PROVISION OF CLUBS: TOP TEN COUNTIES

|  | *No. of Clubs* | *% of total* |
|---|---|---|
| Greater London | 41 | 8.3 |
| Kent | 26 | 5.3 |
| Essex | 19 | 3.8 |
| Hampshire | 19 | 3.8 |
| Sussex | 18 | 3.6 |
| Surrey | 16 | 3.2 |
| West Midlands | 17 | 3.4 |
| Lancashire | 15 | 3.0 |
| Greater Manchester | 15 | 3.0 |
| Hertfordshire | 14 | 2.8 |

*Source:* Auto Cycle Union (1976).

one per 11,725. Other counties with high indices include Gloucester (2.22), Dyfed (2.14), Gwent (2.04), Shropshire (1.93) and Hereford/Worcester (1.81). Auto-cycling therefore appears to be one of the most geographically peripheral as well as one of the most localised sports in England and Wales.

This pattern may be partly due to the kind of constraints under which motor-cycling operates. For scrambling, for example, the perimeter distance is rarely less than 1,200 metres, while the use of road surfaces is constrained by the noise disturbance which would exist if events were held in urban areas.[12] This has resulted in road racing being confined to specialised road racing and aerodrome circuits, of which there are twenty-five plus three on the Isle of Man. Relative concentrations of such facilities are found in eastern England, East Anglia (two circuits) having an index of 2.48, the East Midlands (four) 2.40 and Yorkshire/Humberside (five) 2.29. The south-east and the West Midlands — the most urbanised areas of Britain — contain the lowest *per capita* provision with indices of 0.53 and 0.43 respectively. These areas are more prominent in the case of the more space-intensive sport of speedway racing, the subject of the next section.

Table 10.6.   AUTO-CYCLING: PER CAPITA OPPORTUNITY: TOP TEN COUNTIES

|  | *Per Capita Index* | *One club per* | *No. of clubs* |
|---|---|---|---|
| Powys | 8.48 | 11,725 | 9 |
| Gloucestershire | 2.22 | 44,789 | 11 |
| Cornwall | 2.16 | 46,033 | 9 |
| Dyfed | 2.14 | 46,463 | 7 |
| Lincolnshire | 2.06 | 48,268 | 11 |
| Gwent | 2.04 | 48,741 | 9 |
| Suffolk | 2.03 | 48,981 | 12 |
| Shropshire | 1.93 | 51,519 | 7 |
| Hereford/Worcester | 1.81 | 54,935 | 11 |
| Kent | 1.79 | 55,549 | 26 |

*Source of original data:* see Table 10.5.

## Speedway racing

The most spectator-oriented of the motor sports is speedway racing, initiated in its present form in Australia in the 1920s and imported into Britain in 1927. The first leagues were formed in 1929, with twelve clubs in the south and thirteen in the north. By the mid-1930s, however, the number of clubs had fallen to five, and the sport seemed to have all the characteristics of a temporary craze, rather than an established sport.[13] Although speedway racing today is regarded as one of Britain's most important spectator sports (weekly attendances reached around 350,000 in the late 1960s), its history and geography have been volatile. The pattern of the 1930s was repeated in the 1950s with the rapid growth and spatial expansion of clubs followed by an almost equally rapid decline. The situation in

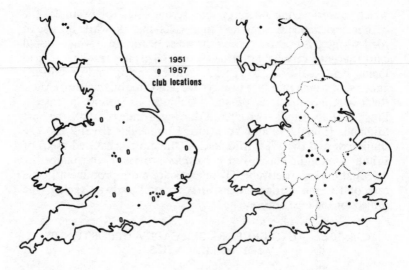

Fig. 10.5. The changing pattern of speedway racing: (*a*) The spatial contraction of speedway activity in the 1950s. With declining demand following the initial post-war craze, only the largest clubs in the strongest markets had survived in 1957. Note that all the 1957 clubs existed in 1951. (*b*) Speedway locations in 1981. (*Sources of data*: (*a*) Carrick, 1977; (*b*) Speedway Promoters Association, 1980.)

the 1950s is summarised in Fig. 10.5*a*. The post-war craze for speedway reached a peak in 1951. Tracks of around 600 – 800 metres in circumference were rapidly constructed in most of the major urban centres with particular clusters in Greater London (seven clubs), the West Midlands and Central Scotland. Some very small towns supported clubs, St. Austell perhaps being one of the more unlikely. Both Long Eaton and Great Yarmouth also had speedway clubs and several larger places remained without them. In the early 1950s, speedway tended to be dominated by one team (Wimbledon), and the growing predicability of results and the dominance of one team contributed to a decline in interest. Clubs in smaller, more peripheral locations closed down and by 1957 only eleven clubs remained — mainly in the larger towns of the south-east and the Midlands. This might be an example of growing spatial rationality in the face of increasing economic constraints.

In recent years speedway has had something of a comeback. Greater stability has been achieved by a reduction in the concentration of power in one or two clubs. This has come about through the restrictive employment conditions of professional speedway riders who are under contract to the league. In this way the league can determine which club they ride for, thus maintaining the element of unpredictability of outcome which is so important if interest in professional sports is to be maintained.

The present distribution pattern of clubs is shown in Fig. 10.5*b*. Of the thirty-six clubs, in two leagues, fourteen are in the south-east and the West Midlands. In *per capita* terms the greatest provision for speedway is found in East Anglia where four clubs give the region an index of 3.19. Other regions with indices of more than 1.30 are the West Midlands (1.39 and five clubs), the north (1.38 and three clubs), and the south-west (1.35 and four clubs). The I.P.C. survey into sports consumption patterns in 1974 revealed that 4.7 per cent of all adults paid to watch speedway racing. In the south-east and East Anglia, however, the figure was 6.4 per cent (this figure excluding Greater London). Areas where speedway is weak are Wales which now has no speedway club, the north-west (index of 0.44) and Scotland (index of 0.55) where only 3.2 per cent of the adult population pay to watch it.[14]

## Basketball

Like speedway racing, basketball is not an indigenous British sport but is an import from the United States. It reached Britain at a time when modern sport was developing rapidly, and Britain was itself exporting many sports all over the world. The importation of sports like basketball exemplifies the apparently insatiable appetite of the British public for new forms of sport — an appetite which is continually whetted and sometimes partly satiated. Basketball had first been played at Springfield, Massachusetts, at the local Y.M.C.A. in 1892,[15] having been invented by Naismith in order to provide indoor recreation for urban youth at times when bad weather precluded outdoor sports. The sport was brought to Britain in 1895 by the physical educationalist, Mme Osterberg, who introduced it to her college in Hampstead.[16] Netball developed from basketball in 1901, and within a year had its own governing body. A sufficient number of basketball clubs existed in Britain by 1922 for national championships to be held, the Central London Y.M.C.A. being a major force at that time. By 1936 thirty-four clubs existed throughout England and Wales.

It is in the 1960s and '70s that basketball has grown significantly in Britain. In 1965, 539 clubs existed with 6,739 individual players; by 1979 868 clubs provided opportunities for 16,495 players. The sport caters primarily for men, only 3,500 women being actively involved in it. Because of the somewhat idiosyncratic administrative regions in which basketball is organised, an analysis of absolute emphasis would be difficult to compare with that for other sports. The West Midlands (i.e. Hereford/Worcester, Shropshire, Staffordshire and most of the metropolitan county of the West Midlands) contains eighty-seven clubs (10 per cent of the total) while Greater London has seventy-five (8.6 per cent) and North Humberside sixty-eight (7.8 per cent). In relative terms a more meaningful pattern can be recognised. Although the highest *per capita* index (2.64) is found in Durham, the most obvious region of above-average emphasis is made up of a band of contiguous counties stretching from Norfolk (2.22) through Northampton (2.05) to Avon. This region consists of counties each of which has more than 1.48 times the national level of provision of basketball clubs (i.e. one club per 53,462 people). Outside this area the only other places with similar levels of emphasis are Durham and Cleveland, Cheshire and Berkshire.

Table 10.7 and Fig. 10.6 clarify the geography of basketball further, but two points are worthy of note. First, although ideally a space-intensive urban sport, the conurbations generally under-emphasise basketball. Norfolk, Northampton and Durham are hardly the places Naismith was thinking of when he conceived basketball as a sport for the urban youth of the American metropolis. Yet in Britain it is in these places in south-central, but not metropolitan England that it most flourishes. Secondly, basketball — unlike many of the sports described so far — cannot be described as southern in orientation. It is tempting to hypothesise that imported sports find greater potential in areas where indigenous sports are relatively weakly developed, but the lack of a one-to-one

Table 10.7.   BASKETBALL. TOP TEN COUNTIES, PER CAPITA

|  | Index | One club per | No. of clubs |
|---|---|---|---|
| Durham | 2.59 | 20,239 | 30 |
| Norfolk | 2.17 | 24,069 | 26 |
| Northamptonshire | 2.00 | 26,110 | 19 |
| Beds. and Cambs. | 1.73 | 30,311 | 32 |
| Avon* | 1.62 | 32,229 | 34 |
| Warwickshire | 1.58 | 33,008 | 24 |
| N.Staffs/S.Cheshire | 1.58 | 33,022 | 23 |
| Cleveland | 1.57 | 33,398 | 17 |
| Berkshire+ | 1.51 | 34,583 | 25 |
| Leicestershire | 1.49 | 35,095 | 22 |

* Includes certain co-terminous districts in Somerset.
+ Includes parts of north Hampshire.

*Source:* English Basketball Association, 1979.

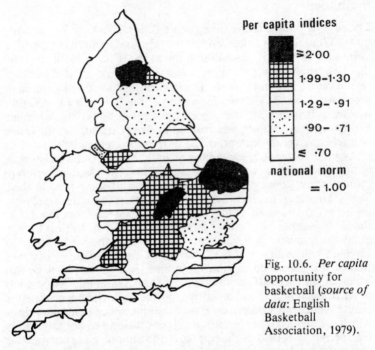

Per capita indices

≥2·00

1·99–1·30

1·29– ·91

·90– ·71

≤ ·70

national norm
= 1.00

Fig. 10.6. *Per capita* opportunity for basketball (*source of data*: English Basketball Association, 1979).

relationship makes this mere speculation, and detailed research into the reasons and methods of adoption of sport in particular places will be the only way of finding out *exactly how* sport develops in time and space.

At its highest domestic level, basketball is played in two divisions of a national league sponsored by Rotary Watches. Indeed, sponsorship has transformed basketball from a sport which is almost entirely participatory-recreational, to one with a strong spectator orientation at the highest level. 250,000 people watched basketball in 1979.[17] At this level the league is dominated by clubs from the south-east of England: in 1979, nine of the twenty-one league clubs coming from this region, giving league basketball a *per capita* index of 1.42 for the south-east. However, one of the vagaries of sponsored sport is that if club sponsorship is withdrawn, the club cannot continue to operate at the highest level against other sponsored clubs. Milton Keynes All Stars, national champions in 1975, were extinct by 1979 following the withdrawal of sponsorship by Embassy cigarettes. The future locational pattern of top-level basketball is therefore likely to be determined as much by the economics of sponsorship as by local population potential or latent demand.

## Swimming

The origins of swimming (like running) as a sport are lost in antiquity. What is known, however, is that the first modern competitive swimming races took place in London in the 1830s, and that in 1869 the first inter-club swimming races took place at the German Gymnasium, also in London. The institutionalisation of swimming was started in 1874 with the formation of the Swimming Federation of Great Britain, but the present governing body, the Amateur Swimming Association, was formed twelve years later as the result of a schism over the interpretation of the word 'amateur'.[18]

As pure recreation, swimming is undoubtedly one of the most popular leisure activities in Britain. Half the population were estimated by Rodgers to have engaged in it at some time in their lives.[19] However, the fact that only 5 per cent of the male population participated in indoor swimming in 1979[20] suggests that interest in the sport may not be as great as was at first expected. Little is known about the number of active swimmers. There are about 1,600 clubs in England and Wales, and the total has fluctuated slightly on either side of this figure during the 1960s and '70s. Yet it is not known which of the clubs affiliated to the Amateur Swimming Association practice swimming as a competitive sport and which ones operate for purely recreational purposes. Hence the analysis of swimming clubs which follows must be treated with some caution and not too readily interpreted as a study of the emphasis on swimming as a competitive sport. Rather, it provides some insights into the geography of opportunities for swimming either competitively or for recreation.

Of the 1,681 swimming clubs in England and Wales in 1979 the main counties in terms of absolute provision were Greater London (230 clubs or 13.7 per cent), Merseyside (103 or 6.1 per cent) and the West Midlands (76 or 4.5 per cent). The top ten counties in terms of numbers of clubs are shown in Table 10.8.

Table 10.8.    SWIMMING CLUBS: TOP TEN COUNTIES IN
ABSOLUTE TERMS, 1979

|  | No. of clubs | % |
|---|---|---|
| Greater London | 230 | 13.7 |
| Merseyside | 103 | 6.1 |
| West Midlands | 76 | 4.5 |
| Lancashire | 66 | 3.9 |
| Kent | 62 | 3.7 |
| Greater Manchester | 58 | 3.4 |
| Hampshire | 56 | 3.3 |
| Essex | 51 | 3.0 |
| Hertfordshire | 48 | 2.8 |
| Derbyshire | 37 | 2.2 |

*Source:* Amateur Swimming Association (1979).

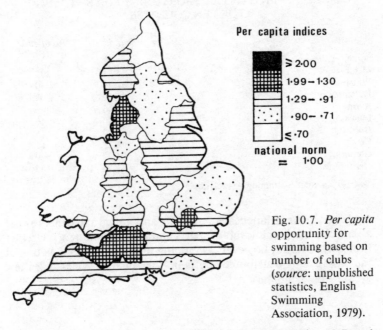

Per capita indices

≥ 2·00
1·99 – 1·30
1·29 – ·91
·90 – ·71
≤ ·70

national norm
= 1·00

Fig. 10.7. *Per capita* opportunity for swimming based on number of clubs (*source*: unpublished statistics, English Swimming Association, 1979).

The *per capita* analysis of swimming clubs (see Fig. 10.7 and Table 10.9) reveals that no county provides opportunities for swimming at more than twice the national level of one club per 29,250 of the population. Indeed, there are only three counties with *per capita* indices of more than 1.5, and most of the country provides opportunites for swimming at around the national average level. The fact that only five counties have indices of less than 0.5 also shows that much of the country is reasonably well provided for. Swimming is a sport which, in comparison with some of the other activities described in this book, exemplifies limited localisation. Of the counties with indices of more than 1.3, those of Somerset-Avon-Wiltshire comprise a 'swimming region' in the south-west while Merseyside-Lancashire is another traditional focus of activity — the English swimming championships having been frequently held at the Derby Baths, Blackpool. The 'outlier' of Hertfordshire is the other county with somewhat above-average opportunity.

Areas of very low emphasis on swimming are confined to Mid- and West Wales, the north-east and a somewhat surprising group of contiguous counties: Buckinghamshire-Oxfordshire-Warwickshire-Staffordshire. Swimming is a sport for which some conurbations are well provided (e.g. Merseyside), others are grossly underprovided

Table 10.9. PER CAPITA OPPORTUNITY FOR SWIMMING:
TOP TEN COUNTIES

| | Index | No. of clubs |
|---|---|---|
| Somerset | 1.95 | 27 |
| Merseyside | 1.91 | 103 |
| Wiltshire | 1.71 | 30 |
| Hertfordshire | 1.50 | 48 |
| Avon | 1.46 | 46 |
| Lancashire | 1.40 | 66 |
| Cornwall | 1.29 | 18 |
| Kent | 1.25 | 62 |
| Cumbria | 1.23 | 20 |
| Derbyshire | 1.22 | 37 |

*Source:* Amateur Swimming Association (1979).

for (e.g. Greater Manchester and Tyne and Wear) and others are at about the national level of *per capita* provision (e.g. Greater London). Overall, however, swimming must be regarded as one of the most evenly distributed sports in England and Wales, with few areas of high emphasis.

## Horse racing

As with sports in which human participation is aided by machines, horse racing might be regarded by some purists as a non-sport. Yet it has acquired a justified reputation as the 'sport of kings', and we may agree with Vanderzwaag that 'it demands physical prowess both by the horse and the jockey'[21] and hence include it as a modern sport.

The social and economic history of the Turf has been described in a scholarly work by Vamplew.[22] He records how before 1840 horse racing was uncommercialised and localised. Although it was a widespread activity for the aristocracy, the horses raced locally because of the limited spatial interaction between regions in the pre-railway age. Some meetings, notably at the small town of Newmarket, in Suffolk, attracted spectators but not horses from outside the local area. Indeed, in the early nineteenth century Newmarket was the Mecca of racing, the result of the Jockey Club having been established there in the 1750s. The formation of this governing body represents one of the earliest examples of institutionalisation in modern sport. Newmarket enjoyed unchallenged primacy in the number of races held there and in the number of horses trained. Out of a total population of 1,200 racehorses, in the early nineteenth century over 400 were trained there.

The railway age revolutionised racing, as it did all sports. As

Vamplew put it, 'all courses within proximity of a station found the spectator catchment area both widened and deepened by the speed and convenience of railway travel',[23] although the extension of a railway line to exclusive Newmarket was viewed as an advantage for the movement of horses more than that of humans. Racing became a national, rather than a local sport. The number of race-courses having more than one meeting per year grew from thirteen in 1848 to thirty-two in 1870. The number of enclosed, rather than open, courses grew rapidly, and from the mid-1870s entrance fees were charged.

Today horse racing is a major sport inasmuch as it not only consumes a large amount of land but also employs a large number of people: as has already been noted, it is also the major sport for gamblers. When stables and their galloping grounds are included, the total area of land associated with horse racing in Britain may be more than 100,000 acres[24]. Vamplew estimated that in the middle of the nineteenth century there were over 100 race-courses in Britain; today, however, there are sixty-one, and decline has also been apparent in patterns of spectatorship. In 1953 nearly 6 million people attended flat or National Hunt races, but by the mid-1970s, numbers had fallen to around 4.5 million. The decline has been less sharp than in football, due perhaps to the greater dependence of racing on middle- and upper-class support. The importance of racing is revealed by some of the figures quoted in Table 10.10. In addition to those listed, other occupational groups associated with it include a large number of veterinary surgeons and nearly 700 amateur riders.

Table 10.10.   INVOLVEMENT IN HORSE
RACING

| Occupational group/activity | No. |
|---|---|
| Spectators | 4,426,000 |
| Betting offices | 13,254 |
| Horses in training | 11,235 |
| Thoroughbred breeders | 6,400 |
| Stable staff | 5,272 |
| Riders | 603 |
| Trainers | 386 |
| Apprentices | 257 |

*Source:* Gill (1975); Rothschild (1978).

Each of the activities listed in Table 10.10 could be analysed geographically. The main concern of this section, however, is to focus on the salient geographical characteristics of horse *racing*, that is to say, the location of courses, meetings and the major races. Race-courses in Britain are not standardised and 'a lot of the peculiar fascination of British racing derives from the enormous variation in size, layout, turf, soil and drainage its courses display'.[25] In addition, considerable variation exists in the intensity of use of courses and the quality of racing witnessed. In any consideration of the location of racing activity, these variations must be taken into account.

In terms of *race-course location*, the south-east is the absolute leader with twelve courses, seven of which are used for both flat and National Hunt events. These race-courses form a suburban ring around southern London, perhaps the best known being Ascot, Epsom, Newbury and Goodwood. Other regions with seven or more courses include Yorkshire/Humberside with eight and the north, the south-west and the West Midlands, each with seven. National Hunt events (races over jumps, held in winter) tend to be characteristic of the northern race-courses while flat racing is more characteristic of the south-west and Midlands. In *per capita* terms, race-courses are most localised in the north (index of 2.00) and East Anglia (1.98). Both regions have around twice as many race-courses *per capita* as the country as a whole (i.e. one per 891,600 people). Other regional indices are shown in Fig. 10.8*a*. Areas with a very low showing in horse racing according to this criterion include the north-west (index of 0.41), Wales (0.61) and the absolute leader in provision, the south-east (0.63).

A more sensitive indicator of regional differences in racing location is found in the analysis of the number of *meetings per year*. These vary considerably between courses, ranging from twenty-three at Windsor to two at Cartmel in Cumbria. In regional terms, the absolute leader is again the south-east with 140 meetings per year, nearly 22 per cent of the total number of 644. The West Midlands, the North and Yorkshire/Humberside also have seventy-five or more meetings per year. Wales, on the other hand, only has twenty and the north-west twenty-four. The *per capita* analysis reveals that the north (2.16) is again the national per capita leader with over twice the national average number of meetings. (i.e. 1 per 84,450). East Anglia (1.59) is again ranked second with the East Midlands (1.52) also having over one and a half times the national norm. Strongly deficient in race meetings are the north-west (0.31), Wales (0.61) and the south-east (0.70). However, race meetings vary in the number of days on which racing is held. For this reason, regional variations in racing activity might best be illustrated by examining the geography of the *number of days racing* per region. In total, 936 days racing should take place in Britain each year. Over 23

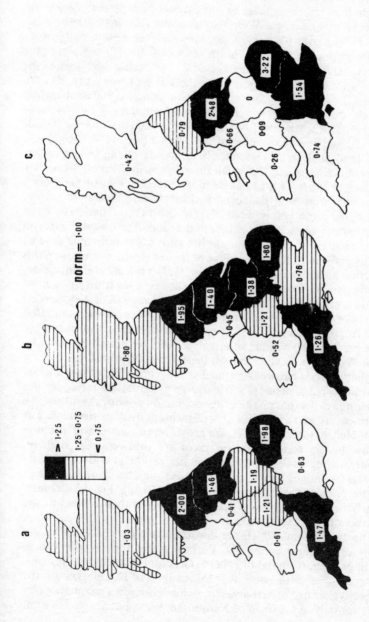

Fig. 10.8. *Per capita* analysis of (*a*) racecourses, (*b*) race days, and (*c*) principal races (*source of data*: Gill, 1975)

per cent (22) of these are found in the south-east, five courses in this region having twenty-three or more days of racing per year. York-shire/Humberside, the West Midlands and the north are the other regions with over 100 days racing. However, the relative patterns are again quite different. The north (index of 1.95) is the *per capita* leader, having almost twice as many days racing per head of the population than the nation as a whole (i.e one day per 58,100). Again, East Anglia (1.80) emerges as a principal focus of racing, largely due to the presence of twenty-four days racing at New-market. The north-west (0.45) and Wales (0.52) both have only half the national average number of days racing (see Fig. 10.8b).

A final analysis of regional differences in racing can be under-taken by comparing the locations of *principal races*. These are defined as those with £4,000 or more added to sweepstakes. Such races represent both the social and economic pinnacle of racing. Again, the south-east is the absolute leader on this criterion with 108 of the principal races, 48 per cent of the total. Ascot alone has forty-three such races, and Epsom, although it holds only nine days of racing per year, has thirteen. Five of the ten top race-courses on this criterion are located in the south-east. Only Yorkshire/Humberside, dominated by Doncaster and York race-courses (thirty-two prin-cipal races) and East Anglia with twenty-four (all at Newmarket) also have over twenty such races. The *per capita* analysis reveals that East Anglia (index of 3.22) has over three times the national average (one per 242,000) number of principal races per head of the popula-tion. When it is recalled that all these are at Newmarket, this East Anglian town is clearly confirmed as the 'capital' of British racing. Yorkshire/Humberside (2.48) is also a very important racing region. It is noteworthy that on this criterion, but on none of the others, the south-east is seen as a major area of racing activity, with an index of 1.54. Hence, while the *per capita* provision of courses and meetings is low in the region, the top races are over-represented there. Contrariwise, while being average *per capita* providers of race-courses or days of racing, the Midlands slump badly when it comes to the provision of principal races (Fig. 10.8c). Fig. 10.8 reveals clearly how principal races are more localised than courses or the number of days racing.

The two regions which are consistently high in the *per capita* analyses of horse racing are Yorkshire and East Anglia. These findings support similar ones in the General Household Survey with respect to spectator patterns.[26] Doncaster and Newmarket are the respective centres of activity, but racing has given a character of its own not only to the town of Newmarket itself, but also to the local landscape.

The wide variety of sports considered in this chapter illustrates the equally diverse locational characteristics of sport, which diverge widely from a normative pattern of equal distribution *per capita*. For example, provision for golf was seen to be strongly concentrated in Scotland and Wales; the location of cycling clubs was less easily generalised, but was relatively absent from many of the southern counties and is relatively (but weakly) localised in a belt stretching from Lancashire to East Anglia. Auto-cycling was described as being geographically peripheral, exemplifying an 'empty heart' of central England. Basketball was more clearly a sport of central England, with few counties in the extreme south or north having above-average *per capita* emphasis; horse racing was strongly associated with East Anglia; but swimming, on the other hand, appeared to have a relatively even distribution pattern, with few counties having very high or very low *per capita* indices.

The locational variety in sports strongly suggests an hypothesis linking sport to local culture. The precise links between sport and place are difficult to unravel, however, and the identification of the patterns displayed in the maps of this chapter are only a first — although vitally necessary — step in identifying the links between sport and the significance it has for people in different places.

## REFERENCES

1. Pottinger (1977).
2. Allison (1980).
3. Dobbs (1973).
4. Howkins and Lowerson (1979).
5. Patmore (1970).
6. ibid.
7. Howkins and Lowerson (1979).
8. Patmore (1973).
9. Aveni (1976).
10. British Cycling Federation (1979).
11. Howkins and Lowerson (1979).
12. Hockin, Goodall and Whittow (1977).
13. Carrick (1977).
14. I.P.C. (1975).
15. Betts (1974).
16. Ivory (1971).
17. Welch (1980).
18. Oppenheim (1970).
19. Rodgers (1967).
20. Central Statistical Office (1979).
21. Vanderzwaag (1972), 62.
22. Vamplew (1976).
23. ibid, 26.
24. Patmore (1970), 222.
25. Gill (1975), 10.
26. Veal (1979).

# 11

## SOME MINORITY SPORTS AND BARRIERS TO ADOPTION

For many people in Britain, the sports which have been discussed in the preceding chapters are of little importance or relevance compared with a large number of minority interest sports. Such activities have few participants and even fewer clubs and facilities. Modern pentathlon, for example has only thirty-one clubs with 470 active participants in Britain.[1] Other minority sports attract few active participants but nevertheless generate a good deal of interest and attract large numbers of fans and spectators. Such a sport is professional boxing.

The fact that the sports described in this chapter are minority interests implies that barriers exist to prevent their being adopted more widely. In some sports, like skiing, rowing and canoeing these barriers are of a physical nature; there are strong locational and site constraints on these activities which means that only certain locations and certain places within particular regions can accommodate them. In other sports the barriers to adoption are of a socio-economic nature. Young men have to be fairly desperate to engage in the precarious occupation of professional boxing. The barrier to the more widespread adoption of pugilism as a profession is affluence and alternative employment, and for this reason we might expect to find a disproportionate number of boxers coming from areas of high unemployment and limited job opportunities. In a sport like rowing, on the other hand, the barrier to more widespread participation may be relative poverty, and we might therefore expect to find this sport localised in areas of affluence. To some extent we have already seen this to be so with tennis (Ch. 8).

With other sports the barriers to adoption are less obvious and may be of a cultural nature. This was seen (in chapter 6) to be true of rugby league. With sports like volleyball and wrestling, however, it is extremely difficult even to hazard a guess at why the geographical patterns of participation are as they are.

The purpose of the present chapter is to examine some of the minority sports from a geographic perspective, focusing on some examples where barriers are of a fairly obvious physical nature and others where reasons for localisation are not so immediately obvious. Examples in this chapter also indicate how the impact of sports technology, in the creation of artificial sporting environ-

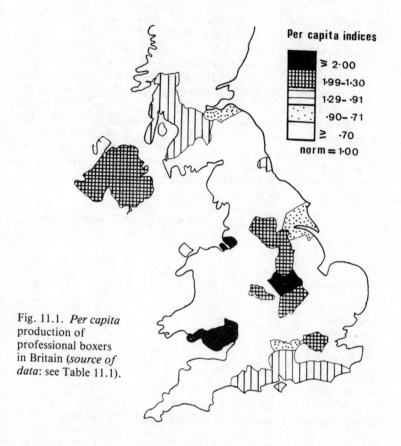

Fig. 11.1. *Per capita* production of professional boxers in Britain (*source of data*: see Table 11.1).

ments, is widening the spatial margins of activity for sports which were previously geographically restricted.

## Professional boxing

Professional boxing is an activity of declining importance, although it is likely that the number of professional fighters has increased from just under 500 in 1979 to over 600 at the time of writing. Economic recessions are likely to increase the number of boxers while full employment is likely to reduce them. In 1952 there were 1,500 professional boxers[2] but by 1979 the number had fallen to 495, 10 per cent of whom were immigrants, mainly from the Caribbean. Fig. 11.1 illustrates the geography of the production of boxers in Britain. Whereas the national level of production is one professional boxer per 125,000 of the population (i.e. an index of 1.00) that for South Glamorgan is one per 29,550 (an index of 4.23). The contiguous counties of Gwent (3.43), Mid-Glamorgan (2.79) and West Glamorgan (2.73) also have well above-average indices of production and confirm that South Wales possesses the dubious distinction of being Britain's premier boxing region. In England a belt of contiguous industrial counties stretching from West Yorkshire to Northamptonshire produces boxers at over one-and-a-third times the national norm, while Liverpool and London are also major foci. It is possible that lack of economic opportunities for the large community of Caribbean origin is 'helping keep the sport alive'[3] in such areas. Professional pugilism has always been perceived as a way out of the ghetto.

Table 11.1.   BOXER PRODUCTION: COUNTIES PRODUCING OVER 1.5 TIMES THE NATIONAL LEVEL OF OUTPUT

|  | *Per capita index* | *No.* |
| --- | --- | --- |
| South Glamorgan | 4.23 | 13 |
| Gwent | 3.43 | 12 |
| Mid-Glamorgan | 2.79 | 12 |
| West Glamorgan | 2.73 | 8 |
| Leicestershire | 2.41 | 16 |
| Merseyside | 2.41 | 30 |
| Northern Ireland | 1.71 | 21 |
| Greater London | 1.66 | 92 |
| West Yorkshire | 1.63 | 27 |
| Nottinghamshire | 1.55 | 10 |
| West Midlands | 1.52 | 12 |

*Source of original data: Boxing News Annual.* Bylbos Publications, 1979.

Table 11.1 and Fig. 11.1 strongly suggest that professional boxers come from areas of limited economic opportunities. In this sense, the geographical pattern of production is similar to that of professional footballers, although noteworthy differences exist. For example, only a limited tradition of professional boxing appears to exist in the north-east, while the East Midlands and London are much more strongly represented.

## The consumption of professional boxing

The production of boxers has been seen to be highly concentrated in certain areas of limited job opportunities, principally in the industrial hearts of England and Wales. In 1978, 989 professional boxing contests took place in Britain and this section looks briefly at the geography of consumption rather than production of boxers. Professional boxing is basically a service confined to about forty-five towns, mainly of sufficient size to guarantee the promoters a sizeable audience. However, some quite large cities failed to provide professional boxing among their service outlets while some places, which at first sight appear rather small to support the sport, put on several bills each year. Table 11.2 indicates the principal centres of British professional pugilism, using the county as the areal unit but indicating also the town or towns within which boxing is undertaken.

Table 11.2.   COUNTIES WITH INDICES OF CONSUMPTION OF
PROFESSIONAL BOXING OF MORE THAN 1.40
*(National norm 1.00)*

|  | *Towns where boxing is staged* | *Index* | *No. of bouts* |
|---|---|---|---|
| West Glamorgan | Aberavon, Swansea | 4.53 | 29 |
| West Midlands | Birmingham, Coventry, | | |
|  | Wolverhampton | 2.96 | 140 |
| Merseyside | Liverpool, Birkenhead | 2.36 | 64 |
| Greater London |  | 2.27 | 275 |
| Gwent | Ebbw Vale, Newport | 1.98 | 15 |
| South Yorkshire | Sheffield, Rotherham, Doncaster | 1.94 | 44 |
| Cleveland | Middlesborough | 1.94 | 19 |
| Hereford-Worcs. | Evesham | 1.76 | 18 |
| Staffordshire | Stoke, Stafford | 1.69 | 29 |
| N. Ireland | Belfast, Derry, Enniskillen | 1.66 | 44 |
| East Sussex | Hove | 1.59 | 18 |
| South Glamorgan | Cardiff, Barry | 1.49 | 10 |
| Essex | Southend | 1.47 | 36 |
| Mid-Glamorgan | Merthyr, Caerphilly | 1.40 | 13 |

*Source of data:* see Table 11.1.

The only non-industrial centres in Table 11.2 are Evesham, Hove and Southend. Apart from these unlikely foci of the boxing subculture, the contents of Table 11.2 suggest that boxing production and consumption are geographically related. However, by no means all the major cities of England and Wales provide professional boxing. Of the metropolitan counties, Tyne and Wear only promoted ten bouts in 1978, while no boxing promotions were held in Bristol, Derby or any Lancashire town except Blackpool. While Greater Manchester witnessed thirty-one bouts, this resulted in a *per capita* index of only 0.67. This suggests that an economic-deterministic explanation of both boxer production and boxing consumption is greatly over-simplified. Despite very similar socio-economic characteristics, the north-east is totally different from South Wales in its pattern of boxing activity. Manchester is very different from neighbouring Merseyside. Boxing *may*, therefore, be more a part of regional, or even sub-regional, culture than *simply* a response to a lack of alternative economic opportunities for young men.

## Olympic wrestling

The sport of Olympic (amateur) wrestling — not to be confused with the Saturday afternoon televised variety — is poorly developed in Britain. It attracts little interest and possesses relatively few clubs, though some growth has occurred in recent years. In 1970 there were fifty-four clubs while in 1979 there were seventy-nine. Of these, twenty-one were members of the Schoolboys Olympic Wrestling Association, and, if schools are excluded, one wrestling club exists for every 926,800 people in England and Wales.

Data on clubs, but regrettably not on numbers of participants, have been provided by the English Olympic Wrestling Association. These allow a *per capita* analysis of opportunity to be undertaken at both the county and regional levels. Because of the very small number of wrestling clubs in most counties, however, an application of the per capita analysis at this scale can give flattering results for small counties with only one club; therefore the *per capita* figures in Table 11.3 should be treated with some caution.

Wrestling is one of the few sports in which the metropolis is not only a major centre in absolute terms but also relatively. Greater London, with its fifteen wrestling clubs, possesses more than a quarter of the national total of senior clubs. In addition it possesses a *per capita* club index of 1.99, twice the national rate. The southeast as a whole is the main wrestling region in absolute terms with twenty-two clubs, 114 senior participants and about 100 schoolboy wrestlers.

Table 11.3.   WRESTLING: OPPORTUNITIES FOR
PARTICIPATION BY COUNTY

| | No. of clubs | Index | | No. of clubs | Index |
|---|---|---|---|---|---|
| Greater London | 15 | 1.99 | West Midlands | 2 | 0.68 |
| Lancashire | 8 | 5.42 | West Glamorgan | 1 | 2.52 |
| Greater Manchester | 4 | 1.38 | Cambridge | 1 | 1.64 |
| West Yorkshire | 4 | 1.79 | Derbyshire | 1 | 1.03 |
| Cleveland | 3 | 3.25 | Avon | 1 | 1.01 |
| Kent | 2 | 1.28 | Surrey | 1 | 0.93 |
| Hertfordshire | 2 | 1.97 | Humberside | 1 | 1.09 |
| Sussex | 2 | 1.45 | Essex | 1 | 0.65 |
| Cheshire | 2 | 2.03 | Merseyside | 1 | 0.59 |

*Source of data:* unpublished statistics provided by the English Olympic Wrestling Association (1979).

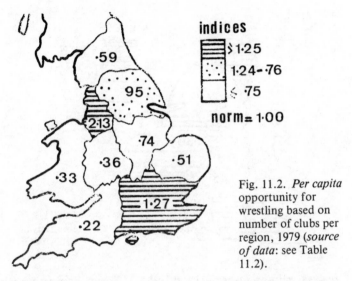

indices

> 1·25

1·24 - ·76

< ·75

norm = 1·00

Fig. 11.2. *Per capita* opportunity for wrestling based on number of clubs per region, 1979 (*source of data*: see Table 11.2).

Because in many counties there are only a few wrestling clubs, or none at all, too much significance should not be read into the data in Table 11.3. A coarser regional sub-division of the country has been drawn up for mapping the geography of wrestling and this is shown in Fig. 11.2. The north-west, with a *per capita* index of 2.13, is the major wrestling region, followed by the south-east with an index of 1.27. Yorkshire-Humberside provide wrestling opportunities at just about the national level, but all other regions are well below it. One cannot begin to explain why the West Midlands should exist as a region of very low wrestling activity between the south-east and the north-west.

Although wrestling is a purely amateur sport, it is remarkable that it has one thing in common with another 'combat' sport already discussed, namely professional boxing. For both sports Greater London is unusual in being a major focus of activity, in both absolute and relative terms.

## Volleyball

Volleyball is a sport that has only recently developed in Britain, the Amateur Volleyball Association was formed as recently as 1955.[4] Like basketball, the game spread from the United States, where it had been developed by W.J. Morgan of the Holyoak Y.M.C.A., Massachusetts, in 1895 as an indoor sport for winter evenings.[5] In England in 1970 there were 105 clubs and 883 players; by 1980, the

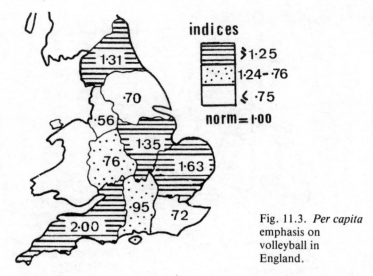

Fig. 11.3. *Per capita* emphasis on volleyball in England.

respective figures were 303 and 1,954. These are impressive increases within only a decade.

One person in 22,340 is a serious volleyball player (i.e. index of 1.00). In both absolute and *per capita* terms the south-west is the major region of emphasis with 370 players and an index of 2.00. East Anglia (which in this sport's administrative regionalisation includes Essex) is the second area of relative emphasis (index of 1.63) while the East Midlands (1.35) and the north (1.31) are the other regions with above one-and-a-quarter times the national average level of emphasis. There are parallels between the geography of volleyball and that of basketball. A comparison of Figs. 10.6 and 11.3 shows that both sports are well developed in a relative sense in East Anglia, the East Midlands and the north. In addition, the north-west and Yorkshire-Humberside are very similar in the relative lack of emphasis on both sports. The hypothesis that American sports imports have different locational characteristics from indigenous sports is a tempting one, but it will not be developed here.

## Canoeing

Although recreational canoeing has been practised in Britain for more than a century, its modern growth as a sport dates from the 1920s when the easily transportable folding canoe was first developed. In 1948, however, only twelve clubs were affiliated to the British Canoe Union.[6] Rapid growth in the 1950s and 1960s produced a total of 370 clubs by 1971 — slightly more than the present

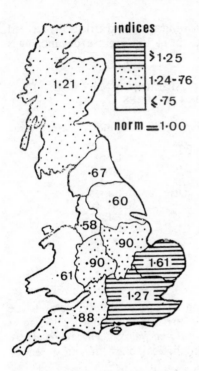

**indices**

≳1·25

1·24-·76

≲·75

**norm = 1·00**

1·21

·67

·60

·58

·90

·90

1·61

·61

1·27

·88

Fig. 11.4. *Per capita* opportunity for canoeing (*source of data*: British Canoe Union, 1979).

total. About half the total number of clubs are 'closed', and only open clubs are dealt with in this section. In 1979 these totalled 129, amounting to one club per 421,000 of the population. Although only six counties in Britain are without a canoe club, the inter- and intra-regional distribution is rather uneven. In absolute terms the south-east is dominant with 32 per cent of all clubs. In *per capita* terms also, the south of England predominates in the provision of clubs. East Anglia (index of 1.61) and the south-east (1.27) are the only regions in England with indices above 1.00. With Scotland as an exception (index of 1.21), there appears to be a gradual diminution in canoeing towards the north, indices falling to below 0.70 beyond the Midlands (see Fig. 11.4).

Within the regions shown in Fig. 11.4 there exists considerable intra-regional variation in opportunity which seems unrelated to the availability on water courses for canoeing. For example, within the south-east, Surrey has a *per capita* index of 3.38 while Berkshire has one of only 0.63; in the Midlands, the West Midlands metropolitan county has an index of 0.62, while Shropshire's index is 2.33. In the north, Cumbria has an index of 2.66, but only one other county has an index above zero. The metropolitan counties all have low indices. Only in the case of Tyne and Wear (0.71) is the index above 0.70. At the county level, the overall national *per capita* leader is Fife (4.96), providing nearly five times the national *per capita* level of opportunity to participate in canoeing. In the northern areas of Britain, canoe activity is almost entirely of the 'white water' variety — canoe racing in swiftly falling streams, the nature of which relates strongly to the physical environment and cannot be artificially constructed. In the south of the country, however, emphasis is placed on flat water racing. Here more gently flowing rivers and artificially created water courses can be used. Indeed, the national centre for canoeing is of this latter type.

Table 11.4.    PER CAPITA PROVISION OF CANOE CLUBS 1979: TEN MAJOR COUNTIES

| County | Per capita index | One club per | No. of clubs |
|---|---|---|---|
| Fife | 4.96 | 84,879 | 4 |
| Surrey | 3.38 | 124,556 | 8 |
| Cumbria | 2.66 | 158,271 | 3 |
| Bedfordshire | 2.58 | 163,178 | 3 |
| Gloucestershire | 2.56 | 164,453 | 3 |
| Norfolk | 2.50 | 168,400 | 4 |
| Buckinghamshire | 2.45 | 171,836 | 3 |
| Shropshire | 2.33 | 180,687 | 2 |
| Sussex | 2.31 | 182,251 | 7 |
| Kent | 2.04 | 206,372 | 7 |

*Source:* as Fig. 11.4.

Overall, however, the location of canoe activity seems to be related more to affluence than to physical environment. It is not a cheap sport, and greatest *per capita* emphasis seems to be where financial resources, rather than physical ones, are most readily available.

## Rowing[7]

The Amateur Rowing Association (A.R.A.) was formed as early as 1882. Traditionally, the sport of rowing has been associated with the upper and middle classes, regattas being a social as much as a sporting event. Oxford and Cambridge universities and the private schools have been the traditional foci of rowing, but in recent years there has been some diffusion down the social hierarchy. In 1939 a total of 240 clubs were affiliated to the A.R.A., but this was not reached again until 1954. By the end of the 1960s, however, the total had risen to 460 — more than half of which were associated with educational institutions.

A number of physical constraints prevent the more widespread adoption of rowing as a competitive sport. About 2 km. of still water is required for rowing, and although twenty-one regattas are held on coastal waters, it is on the nation's major rivers that the sport is mainly found. Canals are generally too narrow; gravel pits are too small; rowing is not usually allowed on reservoirs; and on many rivers motor-boats create a hazard. The River Thames is easily the

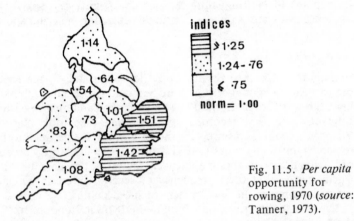

indices

▷ 1·25

1·24 - ·76

≤ ·75

norm = 1·00

Fig. 11.5. *Per capita* opportunity for rowing, 1970 (*source*: Tanner, 1973).

main focus of British rowing activity. There are 128 clubs on the river in Greater London, and one-third of all regattas are held on the Thames. Henley-on-Thames provides the social and sporting highlight of the season.

In absolute terms, the south-east region dominates the provision of rowing clubs. Nearly half the total of non-school clubs are found in the south-east (115 out of a total of 235): apart from concentrations of clubs in London and the Oxford-Reading belt, a number are found around Bedford on the Great Ouse and along the Kent, Sussex and Hampshire coast. The south-west is the second major region in absolute terms, with twenty-two clubs centred mainly on the Bristol area and Exeter region. Other rivers containing minor concentrations of rowing clubs include the Severn, the Trent, the Ouse, the Tyne and the Wear.

In relative terms the south-east of England is also a main centre of rowing, although East Anglia, with concentrations of clubs at Cambridge and Norwich, has a higher *per capita* index than the south-east region (1.51 compared with 1.42). No other region has more than 1.15 times the national *per capita* provision. Fuller details of the regional variations in *per capita* opportunity for rowing are shown in Fig. 11.5. This map is similar to that for canoeing (Fig. 11.4). As it seems likely that there is a large latent demand for rowing, the problem of future provision of rowing facilities is rather serious. Tanner, who has surveyed the problem of facilities for water sports in some detail, feels that the most likely future development may be 'linking a number of wet gravel workings together, for in this way the course may be specifically designed for rowing'.[8] The first still-water course to be developed was in the Trent Valley, at Holme

Pierrepoint in Nottinghamshire, and this facility is shared with canoeing and water skiing as a national centre for the water sports.

## Ice skating[9]

Initially introduced to Britain from the Netherlands in the 1660s, the two early regional centres were Scotland (the Edinburgh Skating Club was formed in the 1740s) and the Fenland area of eastern England. The first recorded speed skating race took place at Wisbech, Cambridgeshire, in the 1760s, and this region has remained the main focus of speed skating in Britain, largely because of its climate and its topographical character. At the same time, it is worth noting that the infrequency of severe winters in England seriously hampers the development of speed skating.

The first skating rinks were built in the 1870s in London. In 1879 the National Skating Association (N.S.A.) was formed in Cambridge, at first as a Fenland organisation for speed skating. With the growth of indoor skating, principally in the London area in the 1890s, however, the administration of the sport moved to the metropolis. The number of serious ice skaters (i.e. members of the N.S.A.) grew rapidly in the inter-war years, having stood at 910 in 1914 and surpassed 2,600 by 1939. Ice rinks, as a sports innovation, were adopted principally in the south-east and in Scotland in this period (Fig. 11.6). The growth of indoor facilities was interrupted by the Second World War, but continued afterwards, albeit slightly more slowly. Most of the early rinks closed soon after they were opened, and eight of the twenty opened between 1920 and 1940 closed in the same period. Some of the post-war rinks have also closed.

Today, thirty-nine ice rinks exist in Britain for the 3,154 members

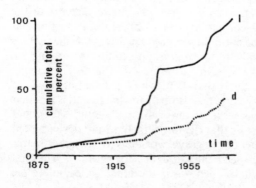

Fig. 11.6. Innovation and 'disinnovation' curves for ice rink construction in Britain (*source of data*: Bird 1979).

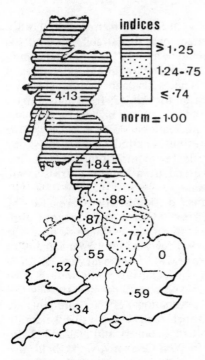

indices

≥ 1·25

1·24 - ·75

≤ ·74

norm = 1·00

Fig. 11.7. *Per capita* opportunity for ice skating based on number of ranks (*source*: see Fig. 11.6).

of the N.S.A. The ratio of one rink per eighty members appears reasonable, but in fact many recreational skaters (non-members) use the rinks, and in Scotland several rinks are used only for curling. In terms of the national population, one rink exists for 1,434,051 people (i.e. index of 1.00). The regional distribution in absolute and *per capita* terms is dominated by Scotland with fifteen rinks and an index of 4.13. Only the northern region, with an index of 1.84, also has an above-average *per capita* provision of rinks. East Anglia, the original centre of the sport, has no indoor facilities, while the two major centres of population — the south-east and the West Midlands, both have only about half the number of rinks for their population potential. The gross under-provision of rinks in the most densely populated parts of the country has undoubtedly retarded the sport, and has meant that Olympic champions such as John Curry and Robin Cousins have had to seek support and facilities in the United States. It is possible, however, that developments in the construction of artificial surfaces may go some way towards equalising the regional distribution of facilities, which, as Fig. 11.7 shows, declines as one moves from Scotland to the south of England.

## Skiing

Like skating, skiing is a sport which has been imported to Britain, having been brought to the attention of the British upper classes by the exploits of the Norwegian, Nansen, at the end of the nineteenth century. Skiing, as a competitive sport, is strongly limited to one or two parts of Scotland as a result of the severe environmental constraints imposed by climate and slopes. Ideally, downhill skiing should take place in a long gully, at least 18 metres wide and 800 metres long, with a drop in altitude over that stretch of about 300 metres. The maximum slope should be about 25 degrees and a minimum of one or two degrees, preferably without abrupt changes in slope angle. A firm snow cover is necessary, and there should be no trees.[10] In Britain the normal season for skiing is from mid-January until the end of April in Scotland, but on the higher slopes it may extend from December to May. Recreational skiing in Wales and the Pennines takes place over a more limited period. Competitive skiing in Britain is limited to relatively few competitions, and several serious British competitors live and train in Alpine areas where conditions are more appropriate.

In Britain the three major areas of skiing activity are all in the Scottish Highlands at Glencoe (Argyll), Glenshee (Perth) and Cairngorm, of which Cairngorm is by far the most developed ski area. The British ski racing calendar for 1981 revealed that from January to April, fourteen Alpine races were held at Cairngorm, six at Glenshee and two at Glencoe. Nordic (cross-country) events were held at Aviemore in the Spey Valley. Skiing is one sport where the physical conditions and the incomes (or occupations) of the contestants are such that British championships are actually held outside Britain. In 1981, for example, the national cross-country and biathlon championships were held at Zwiesel in West Germany, while the British junior alpine championships were at Courmayeur in Italy.[11]

A remarkable post-war development has been the gradual growth in the number of artificial skiing slopes, used largely by recreational skiers. However, the establishment of aritificial ski slope championships suggests that competitive events on artificial surfaces are emerging. The nature of artificial ski slopes varies from indoor slopes to major outdoor slopes of over 400 metres. In Britain the great majority of outdoor dry ski slopes are small, i.e. up to 100 metres. The geographical distribution of these and other dry ski slopes has been charted by Collins.[11]

## Orienteering

Perhaps the most geographical of all sports, orienteering, is a post-war innovation, introduced from Scandinavia in the late 1950s. It grew in significance in the 1960s and by the mid-1970s had become more than a somewhat esoteric recreational activity. By 1977 the total number of clubs had reached 116 and has since grown by about ten per year. Membership of the British Orienteering Federation totals 12,900.

Orienteering may be described as a 'geographical sport' because

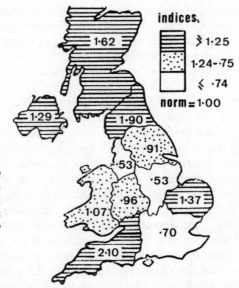

Fig. 11.8. *Per capita* opportunity for orienteering, 1977, based on number of clubs (*source of data: The Orienteer*, 10,2, 1977).

the basic items needed for participation are a compass and a map. Essentially, the sport is an intellectual form of cross-country running, or car rallying without a car.[12] For cross-country orienteering (the most popular form), the length of course is usually between 4 and 12 km. Undulating countryside with a wide range of vegetation cover is the ideal environment. Wooded areas are preferred, since skill in the sport resides in map-reading and orientation, rather than in chasing another competitor who might be easily visible in more open landscapes.[13] Given these physical constraints, one might expect a relationship between *per capita* emphasis and rural upland Britain.

In absolute terms, more than half the 116 clubs are to be found in three regions. The south-east has twenty-four, the south-west eighteen and Scotland seventeen. Within the south-east, the clubs are almost all suburban in location. The East Midlands have only four clubs.

Fig. 11.8 describes the *per capita* distribution of orienteering clubs in 1977. An index of 1.00 represents the national average provision of clubs, i.e. one per 495,400 people. The sport is seen more precisely to deserve being described as geographically peripheral. The highest *per capita* indices are found in the south-west (2.10), the north (1.90) and Scotland (1.62). Northern Ireland and East Anglia also both possess more than one-and-a-quarter times the national average *per capita* provision. Urban England, not surprisingly, tends not to have a strong emphasis on orienteering. The north-west and the East Midlands operate at only about half the national *per capita* rate. Wales is atypical of peripheral Britain in being only an average provider of orienteering clubs.

This chapter has only been able to consider a small number of the many minority sports which exist in Britain today. Because of the small numbers involved, analysis has been undertaken at the inter-regional rather than the inter-county level. It is worth noting, however, that within the regions shown in most of the maps in this chapter, there are marked differences in levels of participation. Some of the sports, notably skating and skiing, and to a lesser degree orienteering, rowing and canoeing, are strongly related to certain physical environmental factors. Others, such as volleyball, are equally localised in particular parts of the country, but here the explanation lies in historical or cultural factors, the full identification of which requires more research. The same is true of wrestling, which is more localised in north-west England than orienteering is in south-west England or Scotland. With boxing it was suggested that economic factors were important in the localisation of the sport, but that cultural factors might also need consideration to explain the relative absence of the sport in areas where, for economic reasons, it might be expected to flourish.

Finally, this chapter has also shown how skiing and, earlier, skating have had their geographical margins extended into areas where, if the natural environment only were considered, they would not exist. The creation of artificial sporting environments may be regarded as innovations in sport, of which the diffusion across time and space is likely to be amenable to the same kinds of analysis as we have undertaken when looking at sports as innovations in themselves.

## REFERENCES

1. Sports Council (1977).
2. I.P.C. (1975).
3. ibid.
4. Anthony (1980), 50.
5. Betts (1974).
6. Tanner (1973).
7. Based largely on Tanner (1973).

8. Tanner (1973).
9. Based on Bird (1979).
10. Hockin, Goodall and Whittow (1977).
11. British Ski Federation (1980).
12. Geographical papers on orienteering include Adams (1972).
13. Hockin, Goodall and Whittow (1977).

# 12
## CONCLUSION: THE GEOGRAPHICAL VIEW

Without the geographical dimension, the study of sport is incomplete. This book has made some initial statements about the geography of British sport. It has shown that there are considerable regional variations in the sports people identify with and take part in; it has highlighted marked regional differences in the 'production' of élite sportsmen and women; it has shown how some areas suffer from underprovision with regard to sports facilities and that there is an inequitable distribution of facilities. Of course, there are many sports which have not been mentioned; this is because of inadequate data and it is hoped that other students will eventually begin to address themselves to the gaps that we have left unfilled here. Many of the findings in this book are invitations to further research. Before considering some of the research directions which sports geographers might begin to follow, some concluding statements need to be made to generalise this book's substantive findings.

Perhaps the most obvious generalisation to be made about the geography of British sport is that to generalise about it is very difficult. It is extremely hazardous to attempt general *explanatory* statements about the geography of sport, although it is not difficult to recognise geographical patterns.

It often happens that the reasons for particular distribution patterns of club locations or for the spatial pattern of participants are tantalisingly far from obvious. Why, for example, should so many more women, per head of the population, play hockey in East Anglia than in the south-east (Fig. 12.1)? Why should more than half the weightlifting clubs in Wales be located in the county of Dyfed, which has only 12 per cent of that country's population (Table 12.1)? A variety of locational *patterns* may be easy to identify, but the *processes* which give rise to those patterns are all too often difficult to establish without careful behavioural or historical research.

What can be said with certainty is that by 1900 almost all British sports — especially the most important ones — were well established; the rules by which they still operate today had been formulated, and the bureaucracies by which they are still administered had been formed. We can represent and summarise the growth of modern sports schematically in the form of a model of sports

164

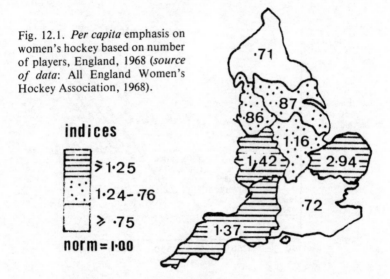

Fig. 12.1. *Per capita* emphasis on women's hockey based on number of players, England, 1968 (*source of data*: All England Women's Hockey Association, 1968).

**indices**

≥ 1·25

1·24 - ·76

≥ ·75

**norm = 1·00**

Table 12.1. PER CAPITA EMPHASIS ON WEIGHTLIFTING IN WALES

| County | Index | No. of clubs |
|--------|-------|--------------|
| Dyfed | 4.38 | 22 |
| Gwynedd | 1.14 | 4 |
| West Glamorgan | 0.87 | 5 |
| Gwent | 0.87 | 6 |
| Mid-Glamorgan | 0.48 | 4 |
| South Glamorgan | 0.33 | 2 |
| Powys | – | 0 |
| Clwyd | – | 0 |
| Wales | 1.00 | 43 |

*Source of original data:* Sports Council for Wales (1975).

development (Fig. 12.2). This shows the change in sports — from unstructured folk games to highly rationalised modern sports — on the left-hand side, with the time-scale shown along the bottom. We have noted that the roots of many British sports lie in the mists of time in the form of folk games, which were later modified by the private schools and universities. Some folk games have continued to the present day — for example, Cumbrian wrestling and Shrove Tuesday football — but on the whole these informal activities have died out. Likewise, some of the private school games, like

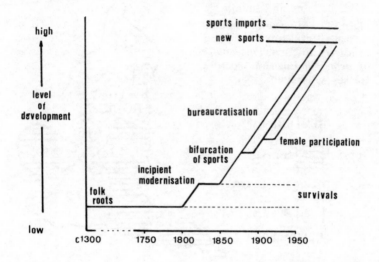

Fig. 12.2.  A model of the historical development of sport
(based on an idea by Dunning, 1975).

the Eton Wall Game, continue in their rough form but as the interest
of only a tiny minority.

The codification of laws and the formation of national sports
associations were the characteristics of the 'take-off' stage of
modern sport. With some sports this stage had been preceded by a
bifurcation, as between rugby and soccer, rugby league and rugby
union, and real tennis and tennis, to mention some of the more
obvious examples. In the late nineteenth century and early in the
twentieth, new sports were invented which had never passed through
a folk game stage — such as the motor sports and table tennis. In
addition, throughout the twentieth century Britain has tried to
satisfy its apparently insatiable appetite for sports by importing a
number of activities, ranging from speedway racing to volleyball.
The other big development of the present century has been the
growing participation of women in sports which were once thought
the preserve of men: tennis and cricket being early examples, and
soccer a more recent one.

The chronology of the development of individual sports, following their formalisation, is similar to that of any innovation. Innovations in sport, in common with those in many other fields, show a slow rate of initial, cautious adoption, after which the adoption process speeds up and finally the rate of growth slows down again until the diffusion process is complete. A number of cumulative adoption curves for individual sports have been included in this book and display a recurring S-shaped pattern.

As sports have developed over time they have also done so over space. Here generalisation is more difficult. It is, however, true that many sports had their roots in southern England, the heartland of the amateur sports ethic. Professionalism, an innovation in sport, is most closely associated with the north of England; it had its origins in the working-class areas of Britain as athletes from these areas strove to compete on equal terms with the more leisured amateurs of the south — a pattern we have seen to be true of soccer, rugby, cricket and athletics. In pre-railway times, it is possible that the spatial diffusion of sport might have occurred in an orderly, neighbourhood-based way. It was suggested that pre-Victorian cricket might be interpreted in this way with its culture hearth in south-east England and progressively weaker areas of emphasis stretching away to the north-west, but following the transport and communications revolution, the diffusion of sports was not spatially restricted, and. outliers of sporting activity were actively colonised well away from the original locations. Of this cricket, again, is the classic case. Other innovations in sport often had their origins in London — as, for example, cinder and synthetic running tracks, indoor skating rinks and public squash courts.

Following the process of spatial diffusion, which with some sports is still going on, a pattern of spatial organisation and regionalisation emerged. The spatial (geographical) patterns of a number of sports have been identified in this book; by mapping the *per capita* distribution of a number of sports attributes, we have been able to identify a number of sports regions. Professional soccer, for example, is largely associated with the north and Midlands, but recreational soccer, on the other hand, seems more of a southern phenomenon, although it is played throughout Britain with very few high *per capita* scores. A similar distribution pattern was seen to exist in swimming and, to a less degree in cycling, with no single region displaying major dominance.

The racket sports were seen to be southern-suburban in character, while motor-cycling was geographically peripheral with an empty English heartland. Basketball, on the other hand, was found to be strongest in south-central England. Other sports have clearly failed to become diffused fully throughout the country due to a variety of

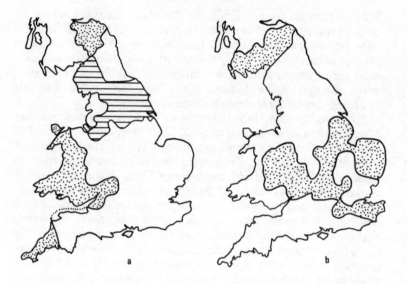

Fig. 12.3. Generalised maps of British sports regions — the examples of (*a*) rugby union (dotted shading) and rugby league, and (*b*) tennis. Shaded areas have more than 1.5 times the national *per capita* number of clubs.

social, economic or physical barriers to more widespread adoption. The consumption by the public of professional boxing, for example, is strongly localised in a few industrial or metropolitan areas; the provision of ice skating rinks is strongly localised in Scotland, while wrestling is twice as important in the north-west as in the country as a whole. Canoeing and rowing both show patterns of south-eastern dominance.

British conurbations generally show a weak emphasis on sports. At the same time they tend to be strong in the production of professional sportsmen in the areas of soccer and boxing. Inevitably, however, both these statements are too sweeping: Merseyside, for example, provides an average number of tennis clubs *per capita* while Manchester provides relatively few boxers. One of the fascinations of sports geography is the discovery of the unexpected regional anomaly which makes prediction and generalisation so difficult. Where a number of contiguous counties possess *per capita* indices above, say, 1.5, we can generalise the pattern of county emphasis and produce general maps showing the regions in which individual sports are strongly localised. Fig. 12.3 provides some examples.

From the perspective of planning for sport we have highlighted the geographical variations in the sports interests, sports provision and sports productivity of different places and regions. Inequalities in provision need to be identified for all sports. For those sports for which there is a country wide demand, the equalisation of opportunity should be an important aim of central government. In our cities and major conurbations, many of which have been seen to be under-provided with sports clubs and facilities, greater opportunity could be achieved if multi-purpose use were made of schools, colleges and other educational facilities. That these should be closed for much of the year is a disgrace for a country which prides itself on its 'Sport for All' attitude. The spatial pattern of professional sport is also in need of reorganisation. The national sport, football, possesses a locotion pattern fashioned in the years of the industrial revolution, and seems quite impervious to the logical pressures to rationalise itself. The opening up of new markets in new towns and the relocation of clubs to areas of greater economic potential should at least be investigated rather than dismissed as unreal.

The geography of sport, besides highlighting sub-optimal or inequitable patterns of provision, also highlights patterns of culture, of a different kind to those studied traditionally by cultural geographers. Sport is a form of mass or popular culture, and Goodey has drawn attention to the fact that in geography we have tended to identify cultural regions with criteria which are no longer relevant to the majority of the population.[1] In an era of increasing cultural homogeneity we may have to look to forms of popular culture in order to identify regions which have real meaning for people. The differences in attachment to sport are more than mere differences in economic opportunity. Areas of declining industry, for example, respond in quite different ways to sports involvement. The northeast fails to produce boxers but it is prolific in the production of soccer players; more prosperous Surrey seems to emphasise racket sports but neighbouring Hampshire does not. Thus, while by many traditional cultural criteria such as religion and language regional boundaries begin to collapse, 'evidence for the persistence of the region in popular culture comes from a number of sources'[2], and one of the most significant of these is sport. It may be that sport goes some way towards resolving what Coull has described as 'the crisis of identity that faces many communities and societies'[3] in the late twentieth century. Few people who have supported Wales at Cardiff Arms Park or Liverpool at Anfield could deny this.

## Some research directions

We have attempted to bring some organisation to a hitherto unorganised body of information — the geography of British sport. Yet in order to complete the task started here, much needs to be done. In post-industrial society, at least three things seem to be happening in sport, each with a geographical dimension demanding investigation. First, there is a great increase in the number of sports enthusiasts; secondly, there is an increase in the proportion of the population who actively participate; and thirdly, there is an increase in the number of sports being practised.[4] Studies of the ways new sports spread geographically would be fascinating analyses of cultural-geographic diffusion; the identification of the barriers to the more widespread development and adoption of women's sports is another priority. Regional variations in sports participation at the school level constitute a topic where British studies fall far behind those undertaken in the United States. *Reasons* why some places are strong in certain sports cannot be inferred from the macro-scale patterns provided in this book, and it may be that behavioural approaches at the micro-scale would be the best way of explaining fully the regional differences in emphasis on particular sports. After all, it is *people* who decide to establish sports in particular places and who decide not to establish them in others.

The effect of sport on peoples' feeling for place and their relationship with the environment is another geographical avenue along which work might proceed. Success in sport certainly generates a change in the view people have of the places in which they live. Sunderland's surprise win in the F.A. Cup of 1973 and its positive effect on people's pride in their own place has been briefly examined by Derrick and McRory, but this remains a strangely isolated piece of work.[5] We also know very little of the effect of *place* on performance. It is clear that in many sports victories are more common at home than away — at least at the commercial-consumer level. This can be attributed partly to concepts of territoriality and 'sense of place' but, as Edwards points out, 'very little information about the details of performance or the distance of a player from his or her home is collected or even recorded by sports statisticians.'[6] We know even less about the effect of participation in sport on the emotional feelings of participants for place and environment. 'Most runners', writes the geographer-marathon runner, Christopher Winters, 'would admit to an esthetic, sensual component in their running. [. . .] Long-distance running induces intermittent but sometimes intense and pleasurable awareness of the environment.'[7] The same seems likely to be true of sports like skiing and orienteering, but the links between participation in sport and awareness, appreciation or experience of place and landscape is a potentially vast area of enquiry, the foundations of which have, till now, scarcely been laid.

In the early 1970s, Rooney concluded his seminal work on the geography of American sport by stating that 'in-depth studies of all sports, particularly with a *world* perspective, are vitally needed'.[8] Here we have been concerned with sport in Britain. What of Britain's place in the world of sport? To date, studies which have tried to measure success in international sport have been over-dependent on analyses of the results of one competition — the Olympic Games, a latter-day religious festival of over-inflated importance.[9] Concentration on the performance of countries in Olympic competition means that vast numbers of élite athletes are ignored and that no accurate in-depth picture of nations' sports outputs can be obtained. Little advance has been made on Jokl's early work on correlating Olympic success (based on the ranking of participants of different countries in each event) with a number of independent variables.[10] There is a need for geographers to apply techniques which summarise regional differences in the 'production' of sportsmen and sportswomen, and which have been widely used in non-sports contexts, to international sports. The kind of work described at the end of Chapter 9 might be extended and applied to a number of other sports. If this were done, a more balanced and more in-depth view of international sport might be obtained.

## Towards an education in sport

Sport pervades society. Given its significance it is not surprising that Vanderzwaag and Sheehan have noted that 'assuming that a knowledge about sport is desirable, we need to devote a part of the elementary and secondary curriculum to the study of sport'.[11] If geographers and other scholars continue their professional involvement in sports studies, sport may eventually be studied, as well as played, in our schools. At the present time, it tends to be used in the classroom, not as a course of study in its own right, but as a means of motivating students in such subjects as economics,[12] geography[13] or ecology.[14] This tends to devalue sport to the level of a teaching gimmick, and serves to reinforce its non-academic connotations. But it is highly desirable in an age of increased time for participatory-recreational sport and the continual bombardment of our senses by media-generated sports images that the serious study of sport be introduced to the school curriculum. Sports studies might occur as parts of individual disciplines (e.g. a 'geography of sport' course within the geography syllabus[15]) or as a new discipline in its own right, manned perhaps by the growing number of sports studies graduates from our institutions of higher education. Vanderzwaag and Sheehan provide some guidance for the design of a school sports studies course, but predictably, due to the limited geographic involvement, geography is excluded.[16] Thompson has shown the illogicality of excluding sport from general studies courses,[17] and it may well be that it is in this context that the study of sport might be introduced to the school curriculum.

In this conclusion a number of reasons why geographers should continue to involve themselves in sports studies have been outlined. In the end, however, it may be that the prime reason is simply that sport is an *interesting subject*, an unfashionable justification for academic study in an age of cries for relevance in research. However, this author hopes that readers will agree with the American cultural geographer, Wilbur Zelinsky, that the geographical patterns in sport are 'exceedingly interesting in themselves. Infatuation with any and all their details is a commendable form of madness'.[18]

## REFERENCES

1. Goodey (1973), 3.
2. op. cit., 6.
3. Coull (1980), 105.
4. Martin and Berry (1974).
5. Derrick and McRory (1973).
6. Edwards (1979).
7. Winters (1980).
8. Rooney (1974), 289.
9. For an interesting analogy between religion and the Olympic Games, see von Kortzfleish (1970).
10. Jokl's (1964) work may be contrasted with that of Levene (1974) and Grimes, Kelley and Rubin (1974) for example.
11. Vanderzwaag and Sheehan (1978), 245.
12. e.g. Ruddock (1979), 70 – 2.
13. e.g. Bale and Gowing (1976).
14. Baker (1977).
15. For some guidance, see Bale (1981*b*).
16. Vanderzwaag and Sheehan (1978).
17. Thompson (1980).
18. Zelinsky (1973), 140.

# APPENDIXES

## A. *The Nystuen-Dacey method of generalising flow data* (p. 42)

Nystuen and Dacey (1961) devised a way of simplifying flow data, such as the inter-regional movement of transferred footballers, to indicate the underlying hierarchical structure of flow movements. The method they used can be exemplified by using the data which formed the basis of Fig. 4.14. If the 302 inter-regional moves were mapped, an extremely jumbled pattern of criss-crossing lines would result. The virtually unintelligible pattern of complex flows across the map can be simplified by initially constructing a matrix (see below) showing both origins and destinations of transferred players.

The accompanying table shows, for example, that fourteen transfers originating from the north-west region were destined for the northern region, while only seven transfers from the north had the north-west as their destination. Other sources and destinations can

### INTER-REGIONAL TRANSFERS OF PROFESSIONAL FOOTBALLERS, 1975 – 1977

|  | *Ireland* | *N. – W.* | *North* | *Yorks./H.* | *E. Midl.* | *W. Midl.* | *E. Anglia* | *S. – E.* | *S. – W.* | *Wales* | *Scotland* |
|---|---|---|---|---|---|---|---|---|---|---|---|
| Ireland | – | 2 | 2 | 1 | 0 | 0 | 0 | 1 | 0 | 0 | 0 |
| North-west | 2 | – | (14) | 13 | 6 | 10 | 0 | 12 | 5 | 1 | 1 |
| North | 0 | 7 | – | 6 | 1 | 5 | 1 | (8) | 1 | 0 | 0 |
| Yorks./Humberside | 1 | 9 | (11) | – | 6 | 5 | 1 | 4 | 2 | 1 | 0 |
| E. Midlands | 0 | 4 | 2 | 8 | – | 3 | 2 | (9) | 1 | 1 | 0 |
| W. Midlands | 0 | 10 | 1 | 6 | (12) | – | 0 | 9 | 1 | 2 | 1 |
| E. Anglia | 0 | 2 | 0 | 0 | 2 | 1 | – | (4) | 2 | 3 | 1 |
| South-east | 0 | 6 | 2 | 7 | (10) | 9 | 6 | – | 7 | 3 | 1 |
| South-west | 0 | 1 | 1 | 1 | 1 | 2 | 2 | (5) | – | 0 | 0 |
| Wales | 0 | 1 | 0 | 0 | 0 | 0 | 0 | 0 | (3) | – | 0 |
| Scotland | 0 | 2 | 3 | 0 | 1 | (4) | 0 | 1 | 0 | 0 | – |
| *Total* | 3 | 44 | 36 | 42 | 39 | 39 | 12 | 53 | 22 | 11 | 4 |
| Rank | 11 | 2 | 6 | 3 | 4 | 4 | 8 | 1 | 7 | 9 | 10 |

*Note.* Intra-regional transfers are omitted.

173

be readily identified in the matrix. The Nystuen-Dacey method identifies the *dominant* flows and simply involves summing all trans-fers to each region, taking note of the region of origin of transferred players, ranking each region on the basis of the number of players it attracts, and then identifying the largest outward flow of players (these are circled in the table). If this flow is to a region which is ranked higher than the region of its origin, it is identified as a dominant flow and is mapped. A simple pattern of linkages identi-fies the importance of certain areas as foci for the movement of transferred players.

## B. *The decentralisation index* (p. 99).

This very simple index quantifies the extent to which a pattern of points (e.g. tennis courts or football pitches) is centralised or decen-tralised within a given area by reference to a central point (e.g. a town centre). The decentralisation index (I) is obtained as follows:

$$I = \frac{(A \times 0) + (B \times 1) + (C \times 2)}{2}$$

where A is the percentage of the total number of points in the most central area; B is the percentage number of points in an intermediate area; and C is the percentage number of points in an outer area. A, B, and C are interpreted in chapter 8 as concentric rings.

A more sensitive index can be calculated if the number of rings is increased. The index ranges in value from 0, denoting extreme cen-tralisation, to 100, denoting extreme decentralisation. It should be stressed that this index says nothing at all about the degree of con-centration or evenness in the distribution of a point pattern. For this, readers are referred to nearest neighbour analysis (Smith, 1977).

## C. *The measurement of athletic specialisation* (p. 124)

In multi-event sports such as track and field athletics, it is desirable to be able to measure the degree to which the 'production' of athletes is specialised or diversified. A number of these indices exist (Ferguson and Forer, 1973), and the one used in this book is perhaps the simplest. It is usually called the I index and, in the context of chapter 9, is given by the square root of the sum of the squared percentage shares of a given region's (country's) athletic output in a given event:

$$I = \sqrt{(P_1{}^2 + P_2{}^2 + P_3{}^2 + \ldots P_n{}^2)}$$

where P is the percentage share of total athletic output in event 1,2,3 etc.

The upper limit of the I scores is always 100, indicating complete concentration of output in one event; the lowest possible score, denoting the most extreme form of diversification (i.e. equal percentage shares of output in each event), depends on the number of events. For eighteen events it is 23.59.

## D. *Combination analysis* (p. 124)

In multi-event sports it may be necessary not only to quantify the degree of specialisation or diversification of output but also to identify which events or event-groups most typify that output. This can be undertaken by the application of combination analysis which can be best exemplified by using the data which arrived at a Sprints-Jumps-Distances combination for France, as was shown in Fig. 9.8.

In order to classify each country, its event-group structures have to be compared with 'model' structures which describe specific descriptive situations. For example, a one event-group country would ideally have 100 per cent of its athletes in one event-group and none in the other three. For a two event-group nation it has 50 per cent in each of two event-groups and none in the rest and for a three event-group nation the percentages would be 33.3, 33.3, 33.3 and 0, and so on. So that comparison may be made easy, the event-group divisions are placed in rank order, and in each case the squares of the deviations from the ideal structures are summed and divided by the number of event groups in each case. Each country is then classified according to the 'model' structure it most closely resembles.

Put another way, the classification is arrived at by the application of statistical variance, which can be defined as $\Sigma\, d^2/N$ where $d$ is the difference between the theoretical and expected percentage of athletes in each event group, and $N$ is the number of event groups. The group that exhibits the minimum variance is the combination that classifies the country. The example of a specific country, France,˙ illustrates this approach. The various calculations in the table overleaf show that France should be classified as a three-event (SJD) country ($\Sigma\, d^2/N = 53.15$).

## CALCULATION OF VARIANCE FOR FRANCE, 1976

| | One-event group | Two-event group | | Three-event group | | | Four-event group | | | |
|---|---|---|---|---|---|---|---|---|---|---|
| | S | S | J | S | J | D | S | J | D | T |
| Actual percentage of athletes | 34.33 | 34.33 | 31.34 | 34.33 | 31.34 | 20.9 | 34.33 | 31.34 | 20.9 | 13.43 |
| Expected theoretical % | 100 | 50 | 50 | 33.33 | 33.33 | 33.33 | 25 | 25 | 25 | 25 |
| $d$ (ignore sign) | 65.67 | 15.67 | 18.66 | 1 | 1.99 | 12.43 | 9.33 | 6.34 | 4.1 | 11.57 |
| $d^2$ | 4312.55 | 245.55 | 348.19 | 1 | 3.96 | 154.5 | 87.05 | 40.2 | 16.81 | 133.86 |
| $\Sigma d^2$ | 4312.55 | 593.74 | | 159.46 | | | 277.92 | | | |
| $\Sigma d^2/N$ | 4312.55 | 296.87 | | 53.15 | | | 69.48 | | | |

$S$ = Sprints; $D$ = Distances; $J$ = Jumps; $T$ = Throws.

# BIBLIOGRAPHY

Aberdare, Lord (1977), *The Royal and Ancient Game of Tennis*, London, Wimbledon Lawn Tennis Museum.

Adams, W.P. (1972), 'Geography and Orienteering', *Journal of Geography*. 71.

Allen, D.E. (1968), *British Tastes*, London, Hutchinson.

All England Women's Hockey Association (1968), *Facilities for Women's Hockey: a Survey*, Women's Hockey Association.

Allison, L. (1978), 'Association football and the urban ethos', *Stanford Journal of International Studies*, 13, 203–28.

——(1980), 'Batsman and bowler: the key relations of Victorian England', *Journal of Sports History*, 7,2, 5–20.

Anthony, D. (1980), *A Strategy for British Sport*, London, Hurst.

Association of American Geographers (1967), *Introductory Geography: Viewpoints and Themes*, Commission on College Geography, Publication 5.

Aveni, C. (1976), 'Man and Machine: Some Neglected Considerations in the Sociology of Sport', *Sport Sociology Bulletin*, 5, 1, 13–23.

Auto Cycle Union (1976), *Yearbook*, London, ACU.

Bailey, P. (1978), *Leisure and Class in Victorian England*, London, Routledge and Kegan Paul.

Baker, R.M. (1977), 'The ecology of association football,' *Bulletin of Environmental Education*, 79, 19–22.

Baker, W.J. (1980), 'The Making of a Working-Class Football Culture in Victorian England', *Journal of Social History*, 13, 2, 441–51.

Bale, J. (1978a), 'A Note on the Geography of Footballers', *Avery Hill College Geography Broadsheet*, 12 (mimeo).

——(1978b), 'Geographical Diffusion and the Adoption of Professionalism in Football in England and Wales', *Geography*, 63, 188–97.

——(1979a), 'The Development of Soccer as a Participant and Spectator Sport; Geographical Aspects,' *State of the Art Review*, Sports Council/ S.S.R.C., London.

——(1979b), 'Track and Field Regions of Europe', *Physical Education Review*, 2, 2, 87–90.

——(1979c), 'A Geography of World Class Track and Field Athletics', *Sports Exchange World*, 4, 26–31.

——(1980a), 'Football Clubs as Neighbours', *Town and Country Planning*, 49, 3, 93–4.

——(1980b), 'Women's Football in England and Wales: a social-geographical perspective', *Physical Education Review*, 3, 2, 137–45.

——(1980c), 'The Adoption of Football in Europe: an Historical-Geographic Perspective', *Canadian Journal of History of Sport and Physical Education*, 11, 2, 56–66.

——(1981a), 'Cricket in Pre-Victorian England and Wales', *Area*, 13, 2,

——(1981b), 'Geography, Sport and Geographical Education', *Geography*, 66, 2, 104–15

——and Gowing, D. (1976), 'Geography and Football', *Teaching Geography Occasional Paper*, 28.

Ball, D.W. (1975), 'A Note on Method in the Sociological Analysis of Sport', in Ball and Loy, 1975, 35–47.

——and Loy, J. (1975), (eds.) *Sport and Social Order; Contributions to the Sociology of Sport*, Reading, Mass., Addison-Wesley.

Barker, D. (1977), 'The paracme of innovations', *Area*, 9, 259–64.

Betts J.R. (1974), *America's Sporting Heritage 1850–1950*, Reading, Mass., Addison-Wesley.

Bird, D.L. (1979), *Our Skating Heritage*, London, National Skating Association of Great Britain.

Bowen, R. (1970), *Cricket: a History of its Growth and Development throughout the World*, London, Eyre and Spottiswoode.

British Amateur Rugby League Association (1979), *Handbook*, Huddersfield, B.A.R.L.A.

British Cycling Federation (1980), *Handbook*, London, B.C.F.

British Speedway Promoters Association (1979), *Directory of Members*, London, B.S.P.A.

Brohm, J.-M. (1978), *Sport: a Prison of Measured Time*, London, Ink Links.

Brookes, C. (1978), *English Cricket: the Game and its Players through the Ages*, London, Weidenfeld and Nicolson.

Buckley, G.B. (1935), *Fresh Light on Eighteenth-Century Cricket*, Birmingham, Cotterell.

——(1937), *Fresh Light on Pre-Victorian Cricket*, Birmingham, Cotterell.

Caine, C.S. (ed.). (1931), *John Wisden's Cricketers' Almanack 1931*, London, John Wisden.

Campbell, C.K. (1971), 'A Locational Analysis of Urban Recreation: adult sports in Bristol', unpublished Ph.D. thesis, University of Bristol.

Cardus, N. (1977), *Cardus on Cricket*, London, Souvenir Press.

Carrick, P. (1977), *Encyclopaedia of Motor Cycle Sport*, London, Robert Hale.

Cashmore, E. (1981), 'The black British sporting life', *New Society*, 57, 977, 215–17.

Central Statistical Office (1979), *Social Trends*, London, H.M.S.O.

Clarke, J. and Jefferson, T. (1976), 'Working-Class Youth Cultures', in Mungham and Pearson, 1976, 141–2.

Clarke, J., Critcher, C. and Johnson R. (eds.) (1979), *Working-Class Culture: Studies in History and Theory*, London, Heinemann.

Coakley, J.J. (1978), *Sport in Society: Issues and Controversies*, St. Louis, C.V. Mosby.

Collins, M.F. (1979), 'Usage, Planning and Management of Dry Ski Slopes: three studies', *Sports Council Research Working Papers*, 14.

Coppock, J.T. (1966), 'The Recreational Use of Land and Water in Rural Britain', *Tijdschrift voor Economische en Sociale Geografie*, 57, 3, 81–96.

Coull, J.R. (1980), 'Cultural Geography — has it a future?', *Area*, 12, 2, 105–8.

Critcher, C. (1979), 'Football since the War', in Clarke, Critcher and Johnson (1979).

Cunningham, J. (1980), 'The Ups and Downs of Sporting Life', *The Guardian*, 3.5.80.

Demmert, H. (1973), *The Economics of Professional Team Sports*, Lexington, Mass., Lexington Books.

Department of Education and Science (1968), *Report of the Committee on Football* ('The Chester Report'), London, H.M.S.O.

Derrick, E. and McRory, J. (1973), 'Cup in hand: Sunderland's self-image after the Cup', *Working Paper*, 8, University of Birmingham Centre for Urban and Regional Studies, University of Birmingham.

De Selincourt, H. (1980), *The Cricket Match*, Oxford University Press.

Dobbs, B. (1973), *Edwardians at Play: Sport 1890–1914*, London, Pelham.

Douglas, P. (1974), *The Football Industry*, London, Howard House.

Doyle, R., Lewis, J.M. and Halmisur, M. (1980), 'A sociological application of Rooney's fan region theory', *Journal of Sports Behavior*, 3, 2, 51–60.

Dunning, E. (1971), 'The Development of modern football', in Dunning, 1971, 133–51.

——(1975), 'Industrialisation and the incipent modernisation of football', *Stadion*, 1,1, 103–39.

——(ed.) (1971), *The Sociology of Sport*, London, Cass.

——and Sheard, K. (1976), 'The Bifurcation of Rugby Union and Rugby League: a case study of organisational conflict and change', *International Review of Sports Sociology*, 2, 11, 31–72.

——(1979), *Barbarians, Gentlemen and Players: a Sociological Study of the Development of Rugby Football*, Oxford, Martin Robertson.

East Midlands Regional Council for Sport and Recreation (1980), *Towards a Regional Strategy*, pt. 2, Resources Report.

Edwards, H. (1973), *Sociology of Sport*, Homewood, Ill., Dorsey Press.

Edwards, J. (1979), 'The home field advantage', in Goldstein, 1979, 409–38.

Eitzen, D.S. and Sage, G.H. (1978), *Sociology of American Sport*, Dubuque, Iowa, W.C. Brown.

English Basketball Association (1979), *Basketball Yearbook, 1979–80*, EBA, Leeds.

English Golf Union (1978), *Yearbook of the English Golf Union*, Wokingham, E.G.U.

English Table Tennis Association (1979), *Address List*, Hastings, E.T.A.

Ferguson, A.G. and Forer, P.C. (1973), 'Aspects of Measuring Employment Specialisation in Great Britain', *Area*, 5, 2, 121–8.

Fitzpatrick, P. (1979), 'Amateur Game is Flourishing', in British Amateur Rugby League Association (1978), 50.

Football Association of Wales (1980), *Official Handbook*, Wrexham, F.A. of Wales.

Gale, F. (1971), *Echoes of Old Cricket Fields*, London, Simpkin Marshall.

Gavin, T. (1979), 'Up from the mines and out from the steelworks? A study of regional variations in the production of top-flight professional footballers in Great Britain', *South Hampshire Geographer*, 11, 22–34.

Gill J. (1975), *Racecourses of Great Britain*, London, Barrie and Jenkins.

Goldstein, H. (ed.), (1979 *Sports, Games and Play; Social and*

*Psychological Viewpoints*, Hillside, N.J., Lawrence Erlbaum Associates.

Goodey, B. (1973), 'Perception of regional identity: some suggestions for broadening geographical exploration in regional context,' *Working Paper*, 12, Centre for Urban and Regional Studies, University of Birmingham.

Greater London Council, 1976, *Greater London Recreation Study*, Part 3, G.L.C.

Green, D.H. (1977), 'Industrialists' information levels of regional incentives', *Regional Studies*, 11, 1, 19—30.

Grimes, A.R. Kelley, W.J. and Rubin, P.H. (1979), 'A socio-economic model of national Olympic performance', *Social Science Quarterly*, 55, 3, 777—82.

Guttmann, A. (1978), *From Ritual To Record: the Nature of Modern Sports*, New York, Columbia University Press.

Harper, W. (1974), 'Philosophy of Physical Education and Sport', in Wilmore, 1974, 239—63.

Harris, H.A. (1975), *Sport in Britain: its Origins and Development*, London, Stanley Paul.

Hockin, B., Goodall, B. and Whittow, J. (1977), 'The site requirements and Planning of outdoor recreational facilities', *Geographical Papers*, 54, Dept. of Geography, University of Reading.

Hodgart R.L. (1978), 'Optimizing Access to Public Services', *Progress in Human Geography*, 2, 1, 17—48.

Hodson, P. (1980), 'Squash', *The Observer*, 10.2.80, 45.

Horn, C. (1975), *Playing Pitches in the Northern Region*, Durham, Northern Sports Council.

Horry, J. (1979), *The History of Squash Rackets*, Brighton, A.C.M. Webb.

Howkins, A. and Lowerson, J. (1979), 'Trends in Leisure 1919—1939', *State of the Art Review*, Sports Council/S.S.R.C.

Inge, M.T. (ed.) (1978), Preface to *Handbook of American Popular Culture*, Westport, Conn., Greenwood Press.

Inglis, F. (1978), *The Name of the Game*, London, Heinemann.

Irvine, D. (1980), 'Cochrane seeks Five-Year Plan', *The Guardian*, 6.11.80, 23.

Ivory, K. (c1971), 'The Development of Basketball in England', unpubl. typescript, University of Birmingham.

I.P.C. (1975), *Leisure*, I.P.C. Marketing Services, 12.

Jackson N.C. (1897), 'Badminton', in Peck and Alflalo, 1897.

Jokl, E. (1964), *Medical Sociology and Cultural Anthropology of Sport and Physical Education*, Springfield, Ill., C.C. Thomas.

Kando, T.M. 1980, *Leisure and Popular Culture in Transition*, St. Louis, Mosby.

Keating, F. (ed.) (1979), *Caught by Keating*, London, Deutsch.

Keating, J. (1964), 'Sportsmanship as a Moral Category', *Ethics*, 80, 1, 25—35.

Konig, E. (1972), 'A Geography of Football in England and Wales', unpubl. B.A. dissertation, Portsmouth Polytechnic.

Kortzfleisch, S. von (1970), 'Religious Olympism', *Social Research*, 37, 231—6.

Lapchick, R.ᴇ. (1975), *The Politics of Race and International Sport*, Westport, Conn., Greenwood Press.

Lawn Tennis Association (1979), *Official Handbook*, London, L.T.A.

Lawson, H.A. and Morford W.R. (1979), 'Ideal Typical Models for Sport', *Journal of Physical Education and Recreation*, 50, 52–4.

Levene, N. (1974), 'Why do Some Countries win Olympic Medals? Some structural correlates of Olympic Games success, 1972', *Sociology and Social Research*, 58, 4, 533–61.

Lewis T. (1980), 'How Essex Rose to Glory', in Preston, 1980, 93–5.

Lovesey, P. (1979), *The Official Centenary History of the Amateur Athletics Association*, London, Guinness Superlatives.

——and Terry, D. (1969), *U.K. Top Ten Year List, 1866*, London, NUTS (mimeo).

Loy, J. (1975), Foreword in Ball and Loy (1975).

Macdonell, A.G. (1935) *England their England*, London, Macmillan.

Macklin, K. (1974), *The History of Rugby League*, London, Stanley Paul.

Magoun, F.R. (1929), 'Football in Medieval England and in Middle English Literature', *The American Historical Review*, 35, 33–45.

——(1931), 'Scottish Popular Football, 1424–1815', *The American Historical Review*, 37, 1–13.

——(1938), *History of Football from the Beginnings to 1871*, Bochum, Verlag Heinrich Pöppinghaus.

Marples, M. (1954), *History of Football*, London, Secker and Warburg.

Martin, T.W. and Berry, K.J., (1974), 'Competitive Sport in Post-Industrial Society: the case of the motor cross racer', *Journal of Popular Culture*, 8, 1, 107–20.

Mason, T. (1980), *Association Football and English Society 1863–1915*, Hassocks, Harvester Press.

McNab, T. (1972), 'History of professional athletics', *Athletics Weekly*, 26, 26, 35 and 37, 16–19 and 26–9.

Meinig, D. (1967), 'Cultural Geography', in Association of American Geographers, (1967), 97–103.

Mikes, G. (1974), 'The Apprenticeship of George Mikes', in Synge, 1974.

Morgan, P.T.J. (1977), 'The Character of Welsh Society', in Thomas, 1977.

Mungham, G. and Pearson G. (1976) (eds.), *Working Class Youth Culture*, London, Routledge and Kegan Paul.

National Union of Track Statisticians (1979), *U.K. Athletics Annual 1979*, London, N.U.T.S.

Newman, O. (1972), *Gambling: Hazard and Reward*, London, Athlone Press.

Nystuen, J. and Dacey, M. (1961), 'A graph theory interpretation of nodal regions', *Papers and Proceedings of the Regional Science Association*, 7, 29–42.

Okrant, M.J. (1977), 'Breadth and Depth in Women's Intercollegiate Athletics: reality or myth?', *Journal of Physical Education and Recreation*, 48.

Oppenheim, F. (1970), *The History of Swimming*, North Hollywood, Cal., Swimming World.

Patmore, A. (1973), 'Patterns of Supply', *Geographical Journal*, 139, 3, 473–82.
——(1970), *Land and Leisure*, Newton Abbott, David and Charles.
Pearson, K. (1979), The institutionalisation of sport forms, *International Review of Sport Sociology*, 1, 14, 50–60.
Peck, H. and Alflalo, E.G. (eds.) (1897), *The Encyclopaedia of Sport*, London, Lawrence and Bullen.
Pickford, R.W. (1945), 'The Psychology of the History and Organisation of Association Football', *The British Journal of Psychology*, 31, 80–93 and 124–44.
Political and Economic Planning (1951), 'The Football Industry', *Planning*, 17, 157–208 and 324–5.
——1956, 'The Cricket Industry', *Planning*, 22, 401, 158–71.
——1966, 'The Football Industry', *Planning*, 32, 496.
Pottinger, G. (1977), *Muirfield and the Honourable Company*, Edinburgh, Scottish Academic Press.
Preston, N. (1953), *Wisden Cricketers' Almanack for 1953*, London, John Wisden.
——(1980), *Wisden Cricketers' Almanack 1980*, London, Queen Anne Press.
Pycroft, J. (1851), *The Cricket Field*, London, St. James's Press.
Quirk, J. (1973), 'An Economic Analysis of Team Movements in Professional Sports', *Law and Contemporary Problems*, 38, 42–66.
Riordan, J. (ed.) (1978), *Sport Under Communism*, London, Hurst.
Rivett, P. (1975), 'The Structure of League Football', *Operational Research Quarterly*, 26, 4, 801–12.
Rodgers, H.B. (1966), *Pilot National Recreation Survey*, British Travel Association/University of Keele.
——(1977), *Rationalising Sports Policies: Sport in its Social Context: International Comparisons*, Strasbourg, Council of Europe, Committee on Sport.
Rollins, J. (ed.) (1979), *Rothman's Football Yearbook*, London, Queen Anne Press.
Rooney, J., (1969), 'Up from the Mines and Out from the Prairies; some geographical implications of football in the United States', *Geographical Review*, 59, 471–92.
——(1974), *A Geography of American Sport: from Cabin Creek to Anaheim*, Reading, Mass., Addison-Wesley.
——(1975), 'Sports from a Geographic Perspective', in Ball and Loy, 1975.
——(1980), *The Recruiting Game*, Lincoln, Neb., University of Nebraska Press.
Rothschild, L. (1978), *Report of the Royal Commission on Gambling, Final Report*, London, H.M.S.O.
Ruddock, L. (1979), 'The Market for Professional Footballers: an economic analysis, *Economics*, 15, 3.
Rugby Football Union (1980), *Handbook, 1979–80*, R.F.U., Twickenham,
Saunders, L. (1972), 'The characteristics and impact of travel generated by Chelsea Football Stadium', in *GLC Department of Planning and Transportation, Research Memorandum*, 344.

Scottish Golf Union (1979), *Official Yearbook*, S.G.U., Glasgow.
Seeley, I.H. (1971), *Outdoor Recreation in the Urban Environment*, London, Macmillan.
Sherriff, R.C. (1930), *Badgers Green*, London, Gollancz.
Sloane, P. (1971), 'The Economics of Professional Football: the football club as a utility maximiser', *Scottish Journal of Political Economy*, 18, 121–46.
——1980, 'Sport in the Market? The Economic Causes and Consequences of the 'Packer Revolution', *Hobart Paper*, 85, Institute of Economic Affairs.
Smith, D.M. (1977), *Patterns in Human Geography*, Harmondsworth, Penguin.
Smith, D. and Williams, G. (1980), *Fields of Praise*, Cardiff, University of Wales Press.
Southey, A. (1897), 'Badminton', in Peck and Alflalo, 1897, 70.
South Western Sports Council (1976), *A Regional Strategy for Sport and Recreation in South West England*, S.W. Sports Council.
Sports Council (1973), *Provision for Sport*, vol. 2, Specialist Facilities, London, Sports Council.
——(1977), *Sport: a Guide to the Governing Bodies*, London, Sports Council.
——(1978), *Directory of Sports Centres and Halls in the United Kingdom*, London, Sports Council.
Sports Council for Wales (1975), *The Situation and Level of Sport in Wales*, Cardiff, Sports Council for Wales.
[Anon.] *Sports Quarterly Magazine* (1980), Running track at Lord's Cricket Ground, 13, 11–13.
Squash Rackets Association (1980), *Affiliated Squash Clubs*, London, S.R.A.
Synge, A. (ed.) (1974), *Strangers Gallery*, London, Lemon Tree Press.
Tanner, M.F. (1973), *Water Resources and Recreation*, Sports Council Water Resources Series, Study 3, London, Sports Council.
Taylor, I. (1976), 'Spectator Violence around Football: the rise and fall of the working-class weekend', *Research Papers in Physical Education*, 3,2, 4–9.
Thaman, R. (1973), 'The Geography of Rugby', unpubl. paper read at annual meeting, Association of American Geographers.
Thomas, D. (ed.) (1977), *Wales: a New Study*, Newton Abbott, David and Charles.
Thompson, K.B. (1980), 'Culture, Sport and the Curriculum,' *British Journal of Educational Studies*, 28, 2, 136–41.
Thornes, J. (1976), 'Rain Starts Play', *Area*, 8, 105–12.
——(1977), 'The Effect of Weather on Sports', *Weather*, 32, 258–67.
Thorns, D. (1973), *Suburbia*, London, Paladin.
Toyne, P. (1974), *Recreation and Environment*, London, Macmillan.
Vamplew, W. (1976), *The Turf*, London, Allen Lane.
Vanderzwaag, H.J. (1972), *Toward a Philosophy of Sport*, Reading, Mass., Addison-Wesley.

——and Sheehan T.J. (1978), *Introduction to Sport Studies: from the Classroom to the Ballpark*, Dubuque, Iowa, W.C. Brown.

Veal, A. (1979), 'Sport and Recreation in England and Wales: an analysis of adult participation patterns in 1977', *Research Memorandum*, 74. Centre for Urban and Regional Studies, University of Birmingham.

Watson, A.F. (ed.) (1903), *English Sport*, London, Macmillan.

Walvin, J. (1975), *The People's Game*, London, Allen Lane.

Weiss, P. (1969), *Sport: a Philosophic Enquiry*, Carbondale, Ill., Southern Illinois University Press.

Welch, M. 1980, 'The Sport of Sponsorship', *Sport and Leisure*, 21, 3, 41.

Welsh Rugby Union (1980), *Handbook, 1979–80*, W.R.U., Cardiff.

White, D. (1977), 'Is county cricket dying?' *New Society*, 44, 820, 651–3.

Wilmore, J.H. (ed.) (1974), *Exercises and Sport Science Reviews*, vol. 2, New York, Academic Press.

Winters, C. (1980), 'Running', *Landscape*, 24, 2, 19–22.

Wiseman, N. (1977), 'The economics of football', *Lloyds Bank Review*, 123, 29–43.

Women's Cricket Association (1979), *Yearbook 1979*, London, WCA.

Young, P. (1971), *A History of British Football*, London, Arrow Books.

Young, B. and Young, L. (1980), *Sport: subcultural perceptions of the footballer, cricketer and rugby footballer*, Occasional Papers in the Psychology of Leisure, 1, Centre for Leisure Studies, University of Salford.

Zelinsky, W. (1973), *A Cultural Geography of the United States*, Englewood Cliffs, N.J., Prentice-Hall.

# INDEX